Women of the Middle Ages

Titles in the Women in History series include:

Women of Ancient Rome
Women of the Civil War
Women of the Middle Ages
Women of the Revolutionary War
Women of the Suffrage Movement

WOMEN
IN
HISTORY

Women of the Middle Ages

Ruth Dean and Melissa Thomson

LUCENT
BOOKS®

THOMSON
™
GALE

San Diego • Detroit • New York • San Francisco • Cleveland • New Haven, Conn. • Waterville, Maine • London • Munich

940.1
DEAN, R

THOMSON

GALE

Cover Image: Copy from a Book of Hours of *Anne of Brittany and Her Patron Saints*.

LIBRARY OF CONGRESS CATALOGING-IN-PUBLICATION DATA

Dean, Ruth, 1947–
   Women of the Middle Ages / by Ruth Dean and Melissa Thomson
      p. cm. — (Women in History Series)
Includes bibliographical references and index.
   ISBN 1-59018-171-9 (hardback: alk. paper)
   1. Women—History—Middle Ages, 500–1500—Juvenile literature. 2. Women—
Employment—History—to 1500—Juvenile literature 3. Civilization, Medieval—
Juvenile literature. I. Thomson, Melissa. II. Title III. Series.
   ML3928.K35 2003
   781.6'8'09—dc21

                                                                    2002011838

Printed in the United States of America

Contents

Foreword

The story of the past as told in traditional historical writings all too often leaves the impression that if men are not the only actors in the narrative, they are assuredly the main characters. With a few notable exceptions, males were the political, military, and economic leaders in virtually every culture throughout recorded time. Since traditional historical scholarship focuses on the public arenas of government, foreign relations, and commerce, the actions and ideas of men—or at least of powerful men—are naturally at the center of conventional accounts of the past.

In the last several decades, however, many historians have abandoned their predecessors' emphasis on "great men" to explore the past "from the bottom up," a phenomenon that has had important consequences for the study of women's history. These social historians, as they are known, focus on the day-to-day experiences of the "silent majority"—those people typically omitted from conventional scholarship because they held relatively little political or economic sway within their societies. In the new social history, members of ethnic and racial minorities, factory workers, peasants, slaves, children, and

women are no longer relegated to the background but are placed at the very heart of the narrative.

Around the same time social historians began broadening their research to include women and other previously neglected elements of society, the feminist movement of the late 1960s and 1970s was also bringing unprecedented attention to the female heritage. Feminists hoped that by examining women's past experiences, contemporary women could better understand why and how gender-based expectations had developed in their societies, as well as how they might reshape inherited—and typically restrictive—economic, social, and political roles in the future.

Today, some four decades after the feminist and social history movements gave new impetus to the study of women's history, there is a rich and continually growing body of work on all aspects of women's lives in the past. The Lucent Books Women in History series draws upon this abundant and diverse literature to introduce students to women's experiences within a variety of past cultures and time periods in terms of the distinct roles they filled. In their capacities as workers, activists, and artists, women exerted significant influence on important events whether they conformed to or broke from traditional roles. The Women in History titles depict extraordinary women who managed to attain positions of influence in their male-dominated societies, including such celebrated heroines as the feisty medieval queen Eleanor of Aquitaine, the brilliant propagandist of the American Revolution Mercy Otis Warren, and the courageous African American activist of the Civil War era Harriet Tubman. Included as well are the stories of the ordinary—and often overlooked—women of the past who also helped shape their societies in myriad ways—moral, intellectual, and economic—without straying far from customary gender roles: the housewives and mothers, school teachers and church volunteers, midwives and nurses and wartime camp followers.

In this series, readers will discover that many of these unsung women took more significant parts in the great political and social upheavals of their day than has often been recognized. In *Women of the American Revolution,* for example, students will learn how American housewives assumed a crucial role in helping the Patriots win the war against Britain. They accomplished this by planting and harvesting fields, producing and trading goods, and doing whatever else was necessary to maintain the family farm or business in the absence of their soldier husbands despite the heavy burden of housekeeping and child care duties they already bore. By their self-sacrificing actions, competence, and ingenuity, these anonymous heroines not only kept their families alive, but kept the economy of their struggling young nation going as well during eight long years of war.

Each volume in this series contains generous commentary from the works of respected contemporary scholars, but the Women in History series particularly emphasizes quotations from primary sources such as diaries, letters, and journals whenever possible to allow the women of the past to speak for themselves. These firsthand accounts not only help students to better understand the dimensions of women's daily spheres—the work they did, the organizations they belonged to, the physical hardships they faced—but also how they viewed themselves and their actions in the light of their society's expectations for their sex.

The distinguished American historian Mary Beard once wrote that women have always been a "force in history." It is hoped that the books in this series will help students to better appreciate the vital yet often little known ways in which women of the past have shaped their societies and cultures.

Introduction:
Vital Contributions to Medieval Society

❦

By the year 500 the Roman Empire was unraveling, with tribes such as the Huns, Franks, Goths, and Vandals invading Europe from the north and east. The centralized government of Rome gave way, and it was left to landowners, who could no longer count on the protection of imperial armies, to administer and defend their own far-flung regions. This was the beginning of the Middle Ages (named by historians who thought of European history in terms of the ancient, middle, and modern eras) or the medieval period (from the Latin *medium,* meaning "middle," and *aevum,* meaning "era"). This period is depicted in books and folklore as the time of knights and ladies, of chivalry and magic, of kings, castles, and cathedrals.

In recent decades, historians have discovered documents and works of art that shed a more realistic light on many aspects of medieval life, including the roles and achievements of women, both poor and wealthy, from all stations in life. The Middle Ages was not just a transition in the history of Europe between the ancient and modern worlds; it was a period with its own distinctive spirit and culture, in which women played vital roles. It would last roughly a thousand years, until Europeans began voyages of exploration in the 1400s and the economic and intellectual growth of the Renaissance gave Europe a new cultural and political identity.

The Medieval Population

By the early Middle Ages, the cities of the former Roman Empire had fallen into disrepair, and most people lived on farmsteads and in small villages scattered evenly across the continent. In the eleventh century the population of Europe was only about 13 million, and though by the fourteenth century it had grown to around 40 million, Europe was still sparsely populated compared with today's population of approximately 727 million.

Disease and poor diet meant that few people survived into old age. Life expectancy for both men and women was under thirty years. Between 1315 and 1322, around 10 percent of the population of

England died from epidemics and malnutrition. Babies and children were particularly vulnerable to illness and starvation; between 12 and 20 percent of children died in infancy, while another 12 to 20 percent died before the age of fifteen.

People of all classes married young, girls at around twelve and boys at around fourteen years old. They had large families—women typically bore six to twelve children—but it was unusual for more than three or four children to survive into adulthood. Alongside the dangers of disease, war, and starvation, in an age when hygiene and sanitation were not understood and the only medicines were herbal preparations, repeated pregnancy and childbirth was perilous for women. Women were particularly at risk between the ages of twenty and forty, when they were weakened by frequent pregnancies and hard manual labor. Those women who survived beyond their childbearing years had a good chance of outliving men, though both men and women who reached the age of twenty could expect to live only to the age of forty.

The Feudal System

When the trade and industry of the Roman Empire died out and cities declined, people turned to the land to make a living. Only 2

Life in a medieval village was strongly affected by disease, malnutrition, and early death.

to 10 percent of the medieval population belonged to the landowning nobility; the vast majority in this agrarian society were men and women peasants, primarily poor farmers tending animals and raising crops. In the medieval era, land represented wealth—the more land a nobleman controlled the more taxes, in the form of farm produce, cloth, and other goods, he could demand from the peasants under his authority. Though the medieval class system was surprisingly flexible, the vast majority of medieval people lived in poverty under rough conditions with limited expectations of improving their lives.

In exchange for their labor, many peasants earned the landowner's protection and the right to raise crops on small parcels of the lord's own land, known as his demesne, and to keep some of their produce. These semifree peasants became known as serfs or villeins, hereditarily bound to the land. They were not free to make their own decisions (they even had to have the lord's permission to marry), to choose the kind of job they wanted, or to move from one manor to another. When the ownership of a manor changed hands, the serfs and their families were transferred along with the land itself.

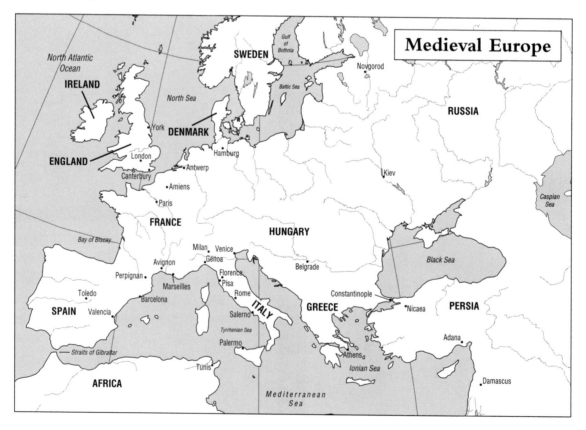

Feudal society also included slaves. St. Patrick first reached Ireland as a slave, having been kidnapped from his home in England by Irish raiders. Some slaves were captured during war or were seized to settle an unpaid debt; many more were born into slavery. Records from the city of Genoa in Italy during the twelfth century show that women were among both slaves and slave owners.

Peasants and serfs made up the lowest level of the feudal system. Above them were knights, who possessed enough wealth to support the powerful warhorse that they rode, wearing heavy armor, into battle. The knights in turn pledged their loyalty and military service to noblemen—dukes, earls and other powerful lords who owned and ruled great estates, advised the ruler of the country, and led armies of knights into battle when necessary. A lord could reward a knight with grants of land, thus enabling the knight to rise to the status of a lord himself. At the top of the system was the king, to whom the nobility pledged loyalty in a ceremony in which the nobleman knelt before the king and placed his hands in the king's.

The feudal system put medieval wealth and power into the hands of a tiny minority of the population. For example, in the late Middle Ages when the population of England was around 5 million, the English nobility consisted of only around one hundred families, who passed their prop-

In feudal society, peasant farmers were bound for their entire lives to the land they tended.

erty and their titles from father to son. This exclusive group of highborn families also enjoyed luxuries and a host of legal and social privileges unavailable to the lower classes. For example, they were recognizable as people of wealth and position not only because they could afford to ride horses and wear expensive clothes but because laws actually forbade peasants from wearing brightly colored or ornamented clothing.

An Era Dominated by the Church

The church, based in Rome and with the pope at its head, was a powerful force in medieval society. Almost everyone in Europe during the Middle Ages was Christian, and religion was an integral part of daily life. The church taught that after death one's soul could rise to heaven, be condemned to a period in purgatory (a place of remorse) before attaining heaven, or be condemned to hell. Men and women, being mortal, could not avoid committing the sins that would condemn them, but the church taught that by praying, confessing their sins, and obeying church laws, people could earn some forgiveness. Better still was to make pilgrimages and give money and land to the church in return for "indulgences," which were assurances of forgiveness for oneself and one's loved ones. Through these gifts of land and money, the church not only became a wealthy and powerful cultural institution but acquired an interest in maintaining the feudal system.

Christian teaching also upheld the feudal system. The church taught that God had brought the social order into being at the time of the Creation, and that by God each person was allotted a position on the social ladder. The privileges and duties of that position were God's will. Consequently, it was a violation of God's will to attempt to step outside one's place in feudal society.

An Era of Warfare and Plague

In the Middle Ages, violent conflict caused serious social upheaval. Across Europe nobles warred against one another to acquire or defend land, or riches, sometimes for many years. The Hundred Years' War, for example, an intermittent conflict between England and France from 1337 to 1453, involved entire societies, from the kings who commanded it to the armies who fought in it to the ordinary people whose taxes paid for it. Abroad, devout Christians went on crusade to free the Holy Land from control by Muslim Arabs. In all there would be nine Crusades, beginning in 1095, in which large armies of men, sometimes accompanied by a few women and even a few noblewomen, left home for long periods. The crusaders sometimes took years to make the perilous journey to Jerusalem, leaving their wives behind to manage as best they could, their return uncertain.

Medieval society was also destabilized by terrible epidemics of plague, or the Black Death. Plague arrived in Europe in the mid–fourteenth century and spread rapidly from country to country. Europeans had no immunity and no effective medicines; some cities lost two-thirds of their populations in one outbreak. The Black

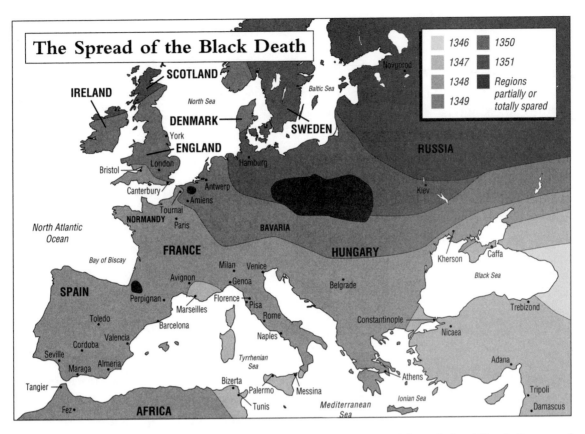

The Spread of the Black Death

Legend:
- 1346
- 1347
- 1348
- 1349
- 1350
- 1351
- Regions partially or totally spared

Map labels: SCOTLAND, IRELAND, Novgorod, Baltic Sea, North Sea, DENMARK, SWEDEN, RUSSIA, York, ENGLAND, Hamburg, Bristol, London, Antwerp, Kiev, Canterbury, Amiens, Tournai, NORMANDY, Paris, BAVARIA, North Atlantic Ocean, FRANCE, HUNGARY, Kherson, Caffa, Bay of Biscay, Milan, Venice, Belgrade, Black Sea, Avignon, Genoa, SPAIN, Perpignan, Florence, Pisa, Marseilles, Rome, Trebizond, Toledo, Barcelona, Constantinople, Nicaea, Valencia, Naples, Cordoba, Seville, Maraga, Almeria, Tyrrhenian Sea, Adana, Tangier, Bizerta, Athens, Tripoli, Palermo, Messina, Ionian Sea, Damascus, Fez, AFRICA, Tunis, Mediterranean Sea

Death recurred every ten to twenty years for about one hundred years, eventually reducing the population of Europe by an estimated 30 percent.

An Era of Superstition and Magic

Beyond religion, medieval women and men had faith in folk medicine and magical properties of natural phenomena. Scientific study in the Middle Ages was based on the theory that all matter was made up of the four "elements"—earth, air, fire, and water—and that all matter, including humans, had four properties—hot, moist, cold, and dry. The balance of these properties was thought to determine people's health, and herbal medicines were chosen according to which of these properties they were believed to impart.

Medieval people also believed in the existence of the Philosopher's Stone, which would change base metals like lead and iron into silver or gold by purifying them. Some people thought that the Philosopher's Stone would transform the base or corrupt qualities of men into noble characteristics. Experimenters like Nicolas Flammel, known as alchemists, spent years in their laboratories trying to find the Philosopher's Stone.

Astrology was important to medieval people, who believed that the movement of the planets in relation to the fixed stars determined the course of daily events. Parents often paid an astrologer to "cast the horoscope" of their newborn children, and the child's trade or betrothed would sometimes be chosen on the basis of the astrologer's predictions.

People of the Middle Ages placed their faith in magic, superstition, and astrology.

Attitudes Toward Women

Women of all classes held an inferior position in medieval society. Women were considered weaker than men in body and mind, and the church taught that they were more sinful, too. Tradeswomen earned less than men doing the same job, and in many cases women were prevented from inheriting property. Women rarely held public office, and they were excluded from universities. Married women were expected to dress modestly, perform their household and family duties diligently, and obey their husbands.

Above all, women were to be quiet. They were taught to listen obediently to the men who held all authority—husbands, fathers, priests—to withhold their own opinions and feelings, and to accept unquestioningly the husband chosen for them.

Women of all classes had little choice about whom they would marry. For noblewomen marriage was often a political matter, arranged by their parents or guardians to increase territory or seal an alliance between two households. Serfs had to have their lord's permission to marry, and their children would be bound to the land, as they were. On some manors there was a specific day each year when the lord or his bailiff (agent) would allot mates to girls who were old enough to marry.

Instructions for Daughters

❧

Eleazer of Mainz, a fourteenth-century German, left a detailed will at his death. Emilie Amt, in *Women's Lives in Medieval Europe: A Sourcebook,* quotes his instructions concerning his daughters' behavior, which reflect the medieval view of women's proper roles:

> My daughters ought not to speak much with strangers, nor jest nor dance with them. They ought to be always at home, and not gadding about. They should not stand at the door, watching whatever passes. I ask, I command, that the daughters of my house never be without work to do, for idleness leads first to boredom, then to sin. But let them spin, or cook, or sew.

The Official Status of Women

Medieval sermons illustrate the attitude of the church and society to women. Preachers criticized women for foolishness and for disobeying their fathers and husbands. They denounced women for vanity in their dress and appearance, for gossiping, and for walking about the village, since women were supposed to stay at home unless their work compelled them to go outside. Husbands were allowed to beat their wives, and preachers encouraged men to do so when their wives were disobedient. In some places, husbands faced fines for failing to beat their wives as punishment.

Medieval law reflects the fact that women were seen as less valuable than men. In many medieval societies, for example, someone who killed another person (whether in an act of murder or by causing an accident) was required to pay a fine. However, in Sardinia, an island near Italy, the fine was fifty pounds for killing a man but only twenty-five pounds for taking a woman's life.

A woman's word was less valued than a man's as well. In two Sardinian towns, for example, a woman's testimony in court was not believed unless backed up by testimony from a man. This practice existed across Europe and as far north as Iceland. There a bishop decreed that, in case of disagreement, a man's word was always to be taken over a woman's.

Despite the low esteem in which they were held, women were a vital part of the medieval economy. Women worked in the fields alongside male peasants and in homes and workshops with craftsmen. Women not only cared for children but taught them the skills they needed to contribute to the family's well-being. Women were skilled workers, traders, and managers. Noblewomen managed large estates, negotiated treaties and marriage agreements, and administered manorial courts. Queens, though they rarely attained the status of kings, sometimes ruled large kingdoms.

Knowing About Medieval Women

As historians research the Middle Ages they rely on the few documents that have survived the centuries, and most records we do have concern the actions of men: legal codes and contracts, financial accounts such as wage payments, land assessments, and tax collections. Documents concerning the life of women in the Middle Ages are rare. Most women could not own land or join one of the trade organizations known as guilds, so they are rarely mentioned in official documents. Few women could read or write—and the process of writing with a quill on parchment was tiresome—so almost no personal journals or letters by women have survived.

However, modern historians have reexamined the remaining records and discovered that much can be learned by new approaches. A great deal of information has been discovered, for example, by searching out women's names in court and account records. Pictures of the lives of women in the Middle Ages appear in legal documents and church writings as well as in medieval fiction, visual art, and the biographies of religious figures. New research has detailed the restrictions that controlled and limited the lives of women, but it also brings to light many exceptional medieval women whose achievements have not been forgotten.

Chapter 1:
Women in the Countryside: Peasants Working at Home and in the Fields

In medieval times, very few women lived storied lives as queens or princesses. The vast majority were peasants, working with their families on large estates known as manors. With their labor, peasant men and women supported the lords and ladies who controlled or owned outright the land where they lived. Most female peasants, however, focused their work on assuring the basic survival of their own families. They were responsible for raising, storing, and preparing much of their families' food, and for making their clothing out of wool and flax. Women in the medieval countryside also worked in the fields, earning wages by doing every type of labor—from thatching roofs to bringing in the harvest—that was needed on the manor. As historian Judith M. Bennett explains:

> Female labor was vital to the rural economy, and some women—either unwilling or unable to marry—had

to survive without the support of a male householder. As a result, medieval countrypeople never thoroughly excluded women from any aspect of economic endeavor. Just as women sometimes held land, so they also labored for wages, and traded at local markets. [1]

Nevertheless, most medieval peasants did marry, and the family was the basic economic unit in the Middle Ages. Typically, the husband was expected to be the head of the family, supporting his wife and children. He was to be the master of the house and all that was within it. Yet, for many reasons, there were frequent variations to this norm, and often a peasant woman bore the responsibility for her household. In one English village, for example, records show that one-fifth of the peasant lands were being cultivated by women. One reason was the high death rate in medieval times. If no son survived, a family's landholding might be inherited by a daughter. In addition, widows often continued to farm, pay rent, and fulfill the obligations associated with their croft, as the small peasant landholdings were called, that were owed to the lord.

Werner Rosener, a German historian, explains that peasants' feudal duties included:

A fourteenth-century painting depicts hard-working peasants.

a wide range of services, such as ploughing, sowing, mowing, harvesting, threshing, corn-grinding and baking. In addition, peasants had to look after the stock of the manor, or they had to build fences, to supply firewood or timber, to drive carts and to run errands. Moreover, their wives and daughters had to do the spinning, weaving and laundry for the demesne farm.[2]

In addition to money, the feudal lord could require payment in the form of grain, wine, chickens and eggs, pigs, sheep, cheese, garden vegetables, honey, wax, flax, linen, wool, or woven textiles.

Another view into the responsibilities of women peasant landholders is presented in a manorial survey of Alwalton, in England, which dates from 1279. A manorial survey is like a census; it is the lord's record of the people living on his manor, their status, and what they owe to him in labor and rent. This survey, of a manor owned by the abbot of Peterborough, lists two widows, both named Sara, who inherited the duties along with the land after their husbands' deaths:

Henry, son of the miller, holds a cottage with a croft which contains one rood [a quarter of an acre], paying thence yearly to the said abbot 2 shillings. Likewise he works for 3 days in carrying hay and other works

Women of the Middle Ages

at the will for the said abbot, each day with 1 man and in autumn one day in cutting grain with 1 man.

Likewise Sara, widow of Matthew Miller, holds a cottage and a croft which contains half a rood, paying to the said abbot 4 pence; and she works just as the said Henry.

Likewise Sara, widow of William Miller, holds a cottage and a croft which contains half a rood, paying to the abbot 4 pence; and she works just as the said Henry.[3]

Entering into Marriage

Once a peasant girl reached her mid- to late teens, she married and entered her husband's household. Because few records were made of peasants' lives, historians debate such general descriptions as a woman's average life expectancy, the number of children she was likely to bear, and so on. Medieval historians estimate that peasant wives were pregnant about half of their adult lives, until approximately age forty, and bore about ten babies, although only one or two would live to adulthood. The information in court records is indirect, and conclusions must be drawn by reading between the lines. According to Bennett:

Aside from the public matters reported in manorial records, no other sources reliably report the experiences of the medieval peasantry. Uniformly illiterate, neither male nor female peasants have left diaries or memoirs that describe their private hopes and values. Living before the time of parochial registration [records kept in a parish church], the medieval peasantry married, gave birth and died without formal written testimony.[4]

In fact, marriage was not established as a church sacrament until the thirteenth century. Before that time, a peasant couple simply stated their intention to marry before their families, with little or no ceremony. The church decreed that girls were of marriageable age at twelve and boys at fourteen, but some studies suggest that peasant children married later than this. Analyzing the manorial court records for the English village of Brigstock, Judith Bennett found that peasants in that community did marry early, however: "Most young people in Brigstock seem to have married within only a few years of first appearing as mature persons before the manorial court."[5] Determining a woman's marital status is difficult in part because not all married peasant women took their husband's last name. In addition, until about 1325, surnames tended to be literal, that is, described a person's occupation rather than her inclusion in a family.

In some countries, the lord of the manor had the right to choose the spouse of a serf, and could separate the couple if he chose to sell one of the serfs to another lord. The nature of the lord's power over the lives of peasants is shown in a document called a customal, dated 1344, from Weitenau, a manor in the Black Forest of Germany. Through the customal, Werner Rosener writes, "The manor claimed the right to force every Christian householder from the age of eighteen or twenty, and every girl from the age of fourteen, into a marriage of the lord's choice."[6]

Typically, however, a peasant woman would marry a man from her own village or a neighboring one, leave her father's household, move to her husband's land, and live under her husband's authority. Unless she was widowed, she would remain in this role for the rest of her life. Judith Bennett explains, "Medieval women stood in relation to the men of their villages as those men stood in relation to manorial administrators; the medieval world was a hierarchical world with peasant women at the bottom."[7]

The Peasant Wife

Sayings and folktales from the Middle Ages show that such expectations of women's subservient role did not always lead to smooth relations in medieval marriage. One proverb cautioned new wives to be obedient: "Let not the hen crow before the rooster."[8] Another medieval adage ruefully conceded, "No man marries without regretting it."[9]

A folktale from medieval England illustrates not only the domestic conflict that sometimes existed between spouses in peasant families but also the scope of a peasant woman's duties. In the "Ballad of the Tyrannical Husband," a wife responds to her husband's complaint about his hard labor in the fields. She recounts a list showing that her own daily tasks are even more difficult.

> The good wife warns him that her day started earlier than his, for she rose to nurse the baby and start the fire. She then milked the cows and took them to pasture and made butter and cheese while she watched the children and dried their tears. Next she fed the poultry and took the geese to the green. She baked and brewed every fortnight [two weeks], and worked on carding wool, spinning, and beating flax [to release the fibers for making linen].

The husband does not believe her, so they switch places the following day.

> When the wife returns from plowing, she finds the children crying, the beer spoiled, the cow not milked, and the husband defeated.[10]

Women of the Middle Ages

The Book of Husbandry

Anthony Fitzherbert wrote *The Boke of Husbandry* in 1523 for other landowners who needed advice on how to manage the work of their peasants. Fitzherbert expected that the estate owner would read selections from this book to the peasants at the appropriate time of year. This advice to peasant wives, whether it was ever in fact read aloud or not, shows the demanding expectations society placed on them:

Thou must make butter, and cheese when thou mayest, serve [feed and care for] thy swine both morning and evening, and give thy poultry meat in the morning. . . . And also in March is time to sow flax . . . and thereof may thou make sheets, broadcloths, towels, shirts, smocks, and such other necessaries, and therefore let thy distaff be always ready for pastime, that thou not be idle. And undoubted a woman cannot get her living honestly with spinning on the distaff, but it stoppeth a gap, and must needs be had.

It is a wife's occupation to winnow all manner of corns [different types of grain], to make malt, to wash and wring, to make hay, shear corn, and in time of need to help her husband to fill the muckwain or dung cart, drive the plow, to load hay corn and such other.

A peasant woman works with her husband on the farm.

Working for the Welfare of the Family

Although it was often undervalued, the work of peasant countrywomen was vital to the everyday lives of their families. Generally, women were responsible for the household tasks, while the men spent most of their workdays in the fields. Yet women did far more than cook and sew.

Their work combined hard manual labor with learned skills. In the days before refrigeration and packaged food, preparing meals was a challenging task that involved storing and preparing the ingredients as well as cooking, which was done over an open fire. To bake bread, for example, many medieval women first had to use a hand mill to grind grain into flour, as well as mixing the dough by hand, kneading it to shape the loaves, and keeping the wood fire burning as it baked.

Women also brewed the beer or ale that was the staple beverage in medieval families, a skilled task requiring knowledge of the many different steps required to malt grain and convert it into the final product. Bennett explains:

> The brewing process took many days and much labor. The grain, usually barley, had to be soaked for several days, then drained of excess water and carefully germinated to create malt. After the malt was dried and ground, the brewer added it to hot water for fermentation. From this mixture, the brewer drained off the wort [the solid part of the malt] and sometimes added herbs or yeast as a final touch. [11]

All of these domestic duties required peasant women to perform a number of outdoor chores. All of the water used by the household had to be carried in from a well, a tiring task, especially in the winter and on laundry days. Women also were responsible for growing a vegetable garden near the house, and they cared for the animals—pigs, cows, and poultry—that provided milk, cheese, eggs, and an occasional meat meal for the family. Away

Milking cows was one of the many duties of the medieval wife.

from the house, it was women's work to gather wild fruit, herbs, greens, berries, mushrooms, and nuts for food.

Responsibilities in the Fields

At harvest time, women joined the men in the fields and performed agricultural work when necessary and at other times as well. Harvesting was exhausting, often dangerous labor, but the community's survival through the winter depended on bringing in the crops before bad weather ruined them. Helena Graham reviewed mentions of women's work in the court cases of the English manor of Alrewas,

1259–1381, to learn about their work in the fields:

> That women would have to do manual tasks on the peasant family holding, interchangeably and alongside men, is evidenced by such cases as that of Adam Hering and his daughter who were presented [before the court] and fined for illegally mowing and reaping a neighbor's meadow.... Women are also presented for failing to enclose their holdings on the common field at the agreed time, for illegally trespassing with animals in the common field, and for illegally blocking the pathways and numerous waterways of the manor. Furthermore, many women were fined for fishing at night and other illegal times, for fishing with illegal nets or for selling fish they had caught without a license. [12]

Certain agricultural tasks generally regarded as "boy's work" were also performed by women and girls, especially when there were no boys in the family. As records of wages tell us, peasant women also worked in the fields for pay.

Heavy Labor in the Fields

Alpaix, a girl born in 1155 in the French village of Cudot, near Paris, is one of the few peasants whose personal history is known today. She spent her last thirty years as an invalid, but she had such beautiful spiritual visions that she was honored with sainthood. As a saint, Alpaix's life story was recorded by a biographer monk, who included some details of what it was like to be a poor peasant girl so long ago. The historian David Herlihy retells Alpaix's early years in his book *Opera Muliebria: Women and Work in Medieval Europe.*

Her father, named Bernard, was a poor man who earned his bread by the sweat of his brow. With the help of two oxen he plowed his little field. As Alpaix was his firstborn, she was called upon to help from the tender age of twelve. Walking ahead of her father, she wielded the goad, pricking the oxen into greater effort. She also carried on her shoulders baskets of manure and of sheep dung to field and garden. Because her arms could not sustain a heavy weight, she was harnessed to a sledge by a rope that passed over her arms and shoulders. Thus she dragged manure to the fields and equaled as best she could the efforts of her father. Her childhood was labor.

They earned money for planting peas and beans, weeding the crops, mowing, reaping grain and binding it into sheaves, threshing (beating the grain to separate the seed from the inedible chaff), shearing sheep, and fishing. Payroll accounts from the city of York, in northern England, list the names of several such women, including Alice Vasour, who was a field-worker, and Elena Wright, who earned money by winnowing, which involves tossing threshed grain in baskets so that the wind blows away the chaff. Once the grain was winnowed, Elena was also responsible for

A woman operates a spinning wheel. Weaving textiles was one of the most important chores of a European family.

selling it in the town market. Another woman, Isabella Horn, who was from the English village of Saham, worked with her husband, Paganus, to gather rushes for making thatched roofs. They took them by boat to sell at the Cambridge market.

The Skill of Weaving

In addition to food, peasant families needed clothing, blankets, sheets, towels, and many other items made of cloth. In the Middle Ages, the two basic sources of fiber for cloth were sheep, whose fleece was spun into wool yarn, and flax, a plant with fibers in its stems that were processed into thread and then woven to create linen. Women played such a significant role in producing these textiles that the distaff, a tool used to spin wool into yarn, became the symbol of women. The distaff appears in the hand of almost every peasant woman shown in medieval visual art, and the term became almost the equivalent of the word woman, as in the phrase "the distaff side," to denote a person's maternal ancestors. The skill of weaving was an important part of women's work; in fact, scholars believe that the word "wife" may be derived from the word "weave."

Marbode, a bishop who lived in Rennes, a town in Brittany (in the northwest part of what is now France), recognized the importance of women's work in producing textiles. He wrote a poem praising women, which includes these lines:

Who draws out the wool and the linen? Who turns the spindle? Who prepares the skein? Who does the weaving? These things done for our benefit are so valuable that, if they were lacking, our life would be less good. [13]

Working for Wages in the Countryside

Many peasant women who had very small landholdings—too small to support a family—earned wages by working in the lord's dairy, milking cows and making cheese and butter. Other women kept a stall at the local market, or earned a small amount by carrying packages to a nearby town and returning with goods to sell. Women who lived near the sea sometimes fished or gathered shellfish from the rocks on the shore. Making butter and cheese brought in a few pence when these dairy products were sold to neighbors. Peasant women also took in lodgers from time to time.

Researchers Marty Williams and Anne Echols found records of enterprising medieval women who sold their goods or services for pay. A fourteenth-century woman named Cardaja, for example, even became quite wealthy by traveling to Florence, Italy, to sell the cabbages she grew on her farm. Williams and Echols also found records of an Englishwoman, Katherine Rolf, who "frequently worked as a day laborer for a convent, earning around two pennies a day for weeding, thatching, making candles, threshing grain, and cleaning wool." [14]

Historian Kathryn Hinds tells of an independent peasant woman in southwestern France who "left her home village and bought a house, farm and vineyard in another village. She kept a flock of sheep and dyed their wool to earn money. During harvest time she and her children worked as hired laborers." [15]

Medieval Servants

In time many medieval women who worked the land as slaves became serfs and then free peasants, with greater ability to choose their work and leave the manor. However, members of the nobility continued to keep slaves as domestic servants in their manor houses and castles. Werner Rosener explains:

There were . . . many bondsmen and bondswomen who earned their living as servants on the lord's home farm or in the manor house itself. They were called *servi* or *manicipia* and had the lowest social status on the estate. They were obliged to be at their lord's service at any time of the day and were fully integrated into the lord's household. [16]

Attended by her servant, a noble lady walks down a street in Chantilly, France.

In contrast with fieldwork, work as a servant was relatively pleasant for the daughters of peasants. Unskilled girls often spent several years working as servants for wealthy peasant families. Many servants were children, beginning to work when they were twelve years of age—and occasionally as young as six or seven. If the girls did not marry, they might continue supporting themselves as servants for their entire lives. The medieval author Alexander Neckham, writing in the twelfth century, wrote a book describing

daily life, including this idealized portrait of two country servants:

> And let there also be a chambermaid whose face may charm and render tranquil the chamber, who, when she finds the time to do so, may knit or unknit silk thread, or make knots, or may sew linen garments and woolen clothes, or may mend. Let her have gloves with the finger tips removed; she should also have a leather case protecting the finger from needle pricks. . . .

> There should also be a serving maid who will place eggs under the sitting hens and will give maslin [mixed rye and wheat] to the geese, and who will feed the ailing lambs with milk from a ewe other than the mother, in her gentleness. She will keep the calves to be weaned, whose teeth are few, in an enclosure by the barn.[17]

Peasant servants lived with the families who employed them, sleeping and eating with the rest of the household. In peasant families, servants were usually treated with respect, although the experience varied with the personalities and attitudes of the people who employed them. For adolescents, entering service could be the equivalent of high school for a teen of today, or it could be a period of drudgery at tasks no one else in the household wanted to do. The historian Barbara Hanawalt quotes the complaint of an unnamed medieval housemaid who had both of these experiences:

> I must serve the old women, I must learn to spin, to wind yarn, to card, to knit, to bleach cloth, and by hand, to brew, bake, make malt, reap, bind sheaves, weed in the garden, milk, serve hogs, make clean their houses; within doors make beds, sweep filthy houses, scrub dirty rags, beat out old coverlets, draw up [mend] old holes. Then to the kitchen, turn the spit, although it was but seldom, for we did not eat meat often; then scour pots, wash dishes, fetch in wood, make a fire, scald milk pans, wash the churn and butter dishes, wring out a cheese cloth, and set everything in good order. [18]

The records of Brigstock, England, give several pieces of information about one servant woman, Agnes Waleys, who

A Romantic View

Even in medieval times, some people romanticized the lives of peasants, seeing them as safe and secure from the pressures faced by women in other classes. One of these was Christine de Pizan, the first woman known to make a living as an author. In *A Medieval Woman's Mirror of Honor,* de Pizan wrote of peasant women:

> Although they are commonly raised on black bread, salt pork and gruel, with only water to drink, and they work very hard, their lives are more secure and more abundant in essentials than the lives of some who are placed very high.

Madonna J. Hettinger suggests that de Pizan's claim was motivated by the hardship in her own life, in Linda E. Mitchell's *Women in Medieval Western European Culture:*

> Christine de Pizan . . . was a young widow with children and in-laws to support and had no large estates at her disposal. Her familiarity with the legal limitations and social burdens placed on women in noble households and her own experience as a widow with few resources other than her social connections and her prose, undoubtedly gave her a critical insider's view of the life of the lady. It was only through that perspective that she could have imagined the peasant woman to have greater security.

came from her native village of Welsa to work in the household of Hugh and Emma Talbot. Agnes was the Talbots' servant for at least five years—possibly eight or more. The close relationship between servant and employer is shown by the fact that the Talbots gave Agnes a house in 1339, of which she would become the owner after their deaths. In 1341 they gave Agnes the right to raise a garden in a certain plot of land.

In all its many forms, the labor of peasant men and women was what made the land productive; it was the basis of all society in the Middle Ages. Werner Rosener explains how labor defined the lives of medieval peasants: "Unremitting toil from dawn to dusk set its stamp on the daily round of peasant work in the home, in the farmyard, in their field or meadows." [19]

As historians trace the evidence of the labor of peasant women, they are establishing its importance to the welfare of the community as a whole, and especially to their families. Tied to the land, peasant women accepted responsibility for feeding and clothing the members of their households, and they also supplied much-needed labor at harvest time, working in the fields. A traditional medieval saying, repeated by mothers to their newlywed daughters, reflects the demanding role they were expected to play: "Dwell at home, daughter, and love thy work much." [20]

Chapter 2:
Women in the Towns and Cities: Skilled Workers and Business Owners

At the beginning of the period now known as the Middle Ages, warfare was common, life was dangerous, and people needed the protection of a feudal lord. By the twelfth century, however, European society was safer and less chaotic, and cities began to grow on trade routes throughout Europe. As Werner Rosener explains: "Most towns ... were founded during the period of rapid urbanization in the twelfth and thirteenth centuries. European society changed to such an extent that towards the end of the phase of economic expansion roughly 10 per cent of the entire population lived in towns." [21]

The lives of urban people were very different from those of medieval peasants, who were bound to serve a feudal lord. One benefit of migrating to a city was the opportunity to escape the hated condition of bondage. After living in one of many medieval cities for a year and a day without being reclaimed by a lord, a person became legally free. Urban life also offered the opportunity to do many different kinds of work. These advantages were especially appealing to women and adolescent girls, who moved to towns and cities in great numbers. This trend was so marked that some cities had a population ratio of one hundred females to only seventy-five or eighty males.

Not limited by the restrictions of the feudal system, the cities and towns of the Middle Ages gradually developed modern economies based on providing services, producing goods for sale, and trade. Playing a significant role in these economies, many city women earned their livelihood with female skills such as housekeeping, dressmaking, and brewing. Some women were mistresses of a craft, managing a workshop and training apprentices and journeywomen. Several medieval women were leaders of large commercial enterprises, and a notable few became wealthy enough to lend money to governments and kings.

The Merchant and Craft Guilds
of the Middle Ages

❧

In the Middle Ages, skilled work was organized by specific craft, with a guild for each type of work. Maryanne Kowaleski and Judith M. Bennett's article "Crafts, Gilds and Women in the Middle Ages" explains how the guilds operated:

Gilds joined together persons engaged in the same trade or craft for their mutual economic, social, and religious benefit. As a rule, only persons involved in skilled work, merchants or artisans, formed gilds, and they controlled access to their work through these organizations. Only members of a gild could engage in the trade or craft supervised by that gild.

Only the "masters" of the gild could maintain workshops, hire apprentices (workers in training) and other workers, and participate in gild politics and decisions. . . . Subject to the control of the masters were trained wage workers, called journeymen or journeywomen, whose wages, working hours, social obligations, and gild privileges were set by the masters and their elected officers. At the bottom of the gild hierarchy were apprentices, adolescents indentured to a master of the gild for a period of about seven years. Masters provided room, board, and training to their apprentices, and when the term of service ended, they sponsored their apprentices' formal admission to the gild as journeymen or journeywomen.

Marian K. Dale's article "The London Silkwomen of the Fifteenth Century" describes the indentures binding two girls to learn this craft. Indentures were agreements between the parents of an adolescent and the master or mistress taking on that person as an apprentice:

The term of service in each case was seven years and the obligations on both sides were similar to those demanded on the occasion of the binding of a male apprentice. It was the girl's duty to cherish the interests of her master and mistress, not to waste their goods, or merchandise . . . to behave well, and not to withdraw unlawfully from their service. For their part her future master and mistress promised to "teach, take charge of, and instruct their apprentice, or cause her to be instructed" in the craft of the wife, to chastise her in meet fashion [to punish her fairly when appropriate], and to find her food, clothing, footwear, a bed, and all other suitable necessaries.

Women in Everyday Occupations

The great majority of urban women had no special training and worked at an everyday occupation. These jobs were low-paying and were not seen as "crafts" —the prestigious, highly regulated occupations that tended to be reserved for men. As Maryanne Kowaleski and Judith M. Bennett explain:

> Women worked at many skilled tasks—as spinsters, brewsters, midwives, cooks, etc.—that were not considered skilled by their contemporaries. In part, this assessment probably reflected a tendency to undervalue women's work; in part, it reflected the fact that such tasks, although skilled, employed skills that were widely available and widely known. [22]

When they came to a city, many girls and women found work as servants. The records of York, England, for example, show that this was the occupation of 20 to 30 percent of the population over fourteen years old. Far more medieval households had servants than do American families today; according to scholar P.J.P. Goldberg, "one-third of urban households . . . may have employed one or more servants." [23] City surveys show that in medieval Germany, as in England, the most common job held by an unmarried woman was servant.

A medieval woman aids her husband in his carpentry business.

Opportunities for City Servants

Some city servants performed household duties, but others were actually employed in workshops. Goldberg explains that medieval individuals who were hired as servants could be working at a variety of tasks: "Service could also be a commercial or craft training that might be valuable subsequently to a young woman, whether married or otherwise." [24]

Migration to a city had another strong appeal for village girls who lacked prospects for marriage. Typically, a medieval girl could not marry unless she had a dowry—land she had been given by her father during his lifetime, land she could expect to inherit, or a sum of money. The poorest families could not afford to provide dowries for their daughters, who therefore would remain unmarried and would probably have to eke out meager livings as spinsters. Becoming a city servant enabled a girl from a poor family to save some of her wages—servants lived with their employers' families—and provide herself with a dowry.

As historian Ann J. Kettle explains, city servants "could acquire useful skills, accumulate their own dowries, and, free from family supervision, conduct their own courtships and enter into late, companionate marriages."[25] A servant girl often had considerable freedom in choosing a mate, unlike a woman in the countryside, whose marriage might be arranged to help her family obtain a piece of land. A peasant girl might find herself, without regard to her own feelings, betrothed at a young age to an older man. In contrast, a city servant could make her own decision about whom to marry. Her employers were also likely to take an interest in her welfare and personal life. Urban families frequently helped their servants choose a spouse and sometimes even held a marriage ceremony for them. Boys worked as servants as well, but they were more likely to be formally apprenticed to craftsmen.

Women Hucksters Selling to the Poor

Other urban women supported themselves by making and selling food or fabric. For example, according to poll-tax records from northern England, Goldberg writes:

> Women as independent traders engaged most frequently in the victualling [food], textiles, clothing, and service sectors of the economy. Indeed a majority of this class of women are probably accounted for by the trades of spinster, carder, huckster, shepster or dressmaker, and laundress. . . . The huckster appears to have been a very general petty trader dealing regularly in foodstuffs but also in cloth, spun yarn or tallow candles. Several of the female traders . . . are surnamed 'huckster,' and a York woman mentioned a coverlet purchased from Magota le Hukkester in her will.[26]

Women with little money became hucksters because this occupation required almost no investment in equipment or materials. Another trade requiring little equipment was candle making. Butchers' and skinners' wives used a byproduct of the slaughtering process, animal fat or tallow, to manufacture and sell candles. Somewhat wealthier were brewsters. These women typically entered this trade when they were widowed and inherited the needed equipment from their husbands. Widows of weavers also frequently continued their husbands' trade; Goldberg mentions one of these, a woman named "Isabella Nunhouse, who inherited her husband's loom." [27]

Women in Skilled Crafts and Trades

As towns grew up, one of the major industries supporting them was the making of cloth. When cloth production moved out of the individual peasant home and into town workshops, many women drew on their skills with textiles to work for wages in these businesses. Some women even set up textile businesses of their own. For example, according to records from medieval Barcelona, in Catalonia (now northeast Spain), "women not only worked the loom, but they were able to own their own shops, giving work to their employees and apprentices." [28]

Medieval laws and customs throughout Europe would seem to have made it

A woman merchant sells roosters in a medieval market.

impossible for women to own a business, yet records from many countries show that some women were able to buy and sell, to borrow and lend money, and to make other types of independent decisions when necessary. Historians believe that many of these women learned a craft from their husbands and also gained from them the business skills needed to buy raw materials, manage apprentices and other workers, and sell the finished goods.

Julia del Grene of York earned wages for carding wool but was also employed in the craft of making saddles with her husband. Women with skills like this, when widowed, frequently carried on the husband's business. In fact, in medieval Florence, a father in a certain trade would often arrange a marriage for his daughter to a man in the same trade. In this way the daughter could take advantage of the skills she had learned while growing up in her father's workshop.

Parisian Women in Trade, 1292

Detailed information about businesswomen in the city of Paris has survived in the form of several tax lists giving the names and occupations of everyone in a trade. In the most complete list, which was compiled in 1292, there were 12,279 entries for people with a man's name, and 2,238 entries, or 15 percent of the total, for women. Some of these women had

atypical occupations, including two "priestesses," a "clergesse," which is the feminine form of the word for clergyman, a blacksmith, and a maker of harnesses. Altogether, the 1292 record lists 172 different occupations for the women of Paris, including juggler and dancer. As David Herlihy points out,

> Women are . . . represented in a large number of trades and in all the principal economic sectors. As drapers [dealers in cloth], money changers, jewelers, and mercers [dealers in silk], they appear among the richest professions. There are even women moneyers, or mint workers. There are copyists and artists. There are women tavern keepers, firewood dealers, and even masons, shoemakers, girdle [belt or sash] makers, millers, smiths, shield makers, and archers. . . . Women were important in the preparation and sale of food. There are five women "friers" . . . five millers, five sellers of milk, four soup makers, four sellers of oil, three brewers, three sellers of cheese, two wine dealers, and several types of bakers. [29]

Herlihy also found records of many women working in the healing professions, in the making of candles, and in all areas of spinning and clothmaking, out of wool, linen, and silk. Eight women were professional embroiderers, six made lace, four specialized in purses, and others created and sold pillowcases, altar cloths, ribbons, and hats.

The social historian Shulamith Shahar also studied the craftswomen of Paris in the thirteenth century. She found records of a woman named Thacia, who received the exclusive right, with her children, to practice the craft of working in leather and leather combined with metal:

> They processed the leather and made leather belts, straps, gloves, shoes and pouches in which seals, silver, documents, prayer missals and toilet articles were kept. In 1287 the monopoly was again granted to a woman, denoted as Marcella. The caskets in whose manufacture women played a part were made of combinations of leather, wood and metal decorations. They also made various purses and scabbards for swords and knives.[30]

Women's Guilds

The women silk workers of Paris organized their work through five different guilds. Although most craft guilds restricted women from participating, or prohibited them altogether, women's silk worker guilds and similar business organizations existed in several other medieval cities as well. As Maryanne Kowaleski and Judith Bennett explain:

Weavers spin silk. This trade proved lucrative for many women.

> The London silkwomen pursued a skilled craft and trade. As throwsters, they turned raw silk into yarn; as weavers, they produced ribbons, laces and other small silk goods; as handworkers, they made up silk laces and other trappings; and as traders in silk, they undertook large and lucrative contracts.[31]

Cologne, Germany, was particularly open to women's businesses, and the city had guilds for women who were spinners of yarn and gold thread, for silk throwers and silk weavers, and for those who produced linen thread.

Linen thread was made from special linen yarn that was dyed blue and carefully treated for quality and usefulness. Apprentices worked under a mistress of

Identifying Medieval Women's Work

In the Middle Ages, many peasants had last names that reflected their occupations. For men, these names often ended in -er. An example is Miller, originally designating a man who operates a mill for grinding grain into flour.

The ending -ster (from a word meaning "woman" in the Old English language) identified a woman's occupation. Today, the word "spinster" still refers to a woman—specifically, this word means "unmarried woman." It is a heritage of medieval times, when women who did not marry often supported themselves with their only marketable skill, spinning, and were known throughout their lives as "spinsters."

Other names that once indicated women's work include:

Baxter, a woman baker

Brewster, a woman who brews beer or ale

Huckster, a woman who sells ribbons, pins, and other small items

Kempster, a "comber," a woman who uses a card, which is a comb with many metal teeth, to straighten the fibers in a sheep's fleece and prepare it for spinning into yarn

Maltster, a woman who manufactures barley malt (sprouted grains of barley), the basic ingredient of ale

Sempster or shepster, a seamstress

Tapster, a barmaid, who uses a tap to draw beer or ale out of a barrel for serving in a tavern

Throwster, a woman who "throws" raw silk to prepare it for weaving

Webster, a woman weaver

A few other women whose surnames indicate how they made their living are Ellen Nurse, Matilda Midwife, and Rose Mustardmaker.

the craft for four years, and at the end of that time a committee of guild members examined their work to judge its quality. If the apprentice passed this inspection, the guild allowed her to open her own workshop. Further, she could set up one daughter as an independent producer with a business in her own name. Guild regulations permitted each workshop to have three girls or servants as helpers.

The production of gold and silver thread and of silk luxury goods also tended to be family affairs in Cologne. Production of metallic thread required two processes, and often the husband would be skilled in the first step, which was to beat the precious metal and stretch it into fine threads. The wife then used her spinning skills to wind the metal threads around a core thread made of linen, silk, or cotton. The historian Margret Wensky explains that the women exported the thread and also used it, within the city of Cologne itself, to embroider "coats of arms and heraldic devices, in braid trimmings and in silk-weaving."[32]

The Women Silk Makers of Cologne

From 1437 to 1504, there were 116 women silk makers working in Cologne. These women were important business leaders in their city, employing a total of 765 apprentices. As Wensky reports,

"The apprentice roll . . . reveals that the silk-makers did not only take on girls from Cologne as apprentices, but from elsewhere as well. The majority came from the Rhineland and Westphalia . . . but others came from Antwerp, Deventer, Nymegen and Lubeck."[33]

One Cologne silk maker was named Fygen Lutzenkirchen. Her husband, Peter Lutzenkirchen, was a merchant who traded with many different European cities. At

A fourteenth-century engraving depicts the busy German city of Cologne, an important center for women's commerce in the Middle Ages.

the trade fairs in Frankfurt and Antwerp, he bought raw silk for Fygen's workers to process into finished goods, which he sold on return trips to the fairs. After her husband's death in 1496, Fygen handed over her silk-making workshop to her daughter Lysbeth and continued to operate Peter's import-export business. In this Fygen was so successful that by 1511 she was one of the richest citizens in the city of Cologne.

Another Cologne silk maker was Tryngen Ime Hove, who headed a very large enterprise known as "zer Roder Duyr" (At the Red Door). Tryngen became an officer of the silk makers' guild in 1462. Wensky explains:

> In the 39 years down to 1501, Tryngen trained 39 apprentices and she was always the employer of the largest number of apprentices in the city. Some idea of the output of Tryngen's shop can be gained from calculating the amount of raw silk consumed, and the customs registers between 1491 and 1495 suggest that she purchased one-fifth, or about 20,000 pounds, of the raw silk that entered the city in those years. On average, therefore, her shop must have been processing about 5,000 pounds of raw silk per annum [each year].[34]

Tryngen's son Mertyn Ime Hove married Lysbeth Lutzenkirchen, and together Mertyn and Lysbeth continued the silk-making businesses built by their mothers. According to Wensky, "At the end of the XVth century the making of silk was one of the most important—if not *the most* important—export industry in Cologne of the period."[35]

Licoricia of Winchester

In medieval times, Jews lived in minority communities scattered throughout Christian Europe. They were sometimes persecuted; nevertheless, both men and women in these communities played an important part in the economies of their regions. Christian teachings prohibited lending money at interest, so Jews often provided this important financial service. Judith R. Baskin has studied the roles of Jewish women in medieval times. She explains:

> Women engaged in all kinds of commercial operations and occupations, but moneylending was especially preferred; widows would frequently continue their financial activities, occasionally in partnership with another woman. Such undertakings, which could be extremely complex, required literacy in the vernacular [the local language, as opposed to Hebrew or Latin] and training in mathematics and bookkeeping skills.[36]

The best-known Jewish woman moneylender in medieval England was Licoricia

The Patron Saint of Servant Girls

One medieval girl who spent her entire life as a servant was St. Zita of Lucca. Her life is known through a biography written in 1859, more than six centuries after her birth in 1218, by Baron de Montreuil, a French nobleman, drawing on notarized statements made shortly after her death. Zita's very poor family lived in the countryside outside of the Italian city of Lucca. She must have realized that her father had no money to give her a dowry; when she was twelve years old, she told him that she wanted to become a servant. Her father took Zita to work for the Fatinellis, who were rich wool merchants in the nearby city of Lucca, where she would live and work for forty-eight years, the remainder of her life.

Having grown up in poverty, Zita was always concerned for the poor and often saved her own meals to feed those who begged outside the door of the Fatinellis' house. She also showed her saintliness by performing her work so diligently. Baron de Montreuil says,

Those who have written of her life speak of the zeal with which Zita aided her fellow-servants: she did not think her task ended, so long as there was a service to be rendered, or any useful thing to be done in the house; but rested from the fatigue of one occupation by performing another.

De Montreuil emphasizes Zita's gentleness and the "singular sweetness" of her voice and says that she avoided the "company, idle conversation, and useless amusements" of the other servants.

This conduct did not, of course, please her fellow-servants; they endeavored, at first, to draw her into their evil habits; furious at their want [lack] of success, they invented a thousand calumnies [lies] against her, representing her modesty and piety as hypocrisy and falsehood. They accused her of endeavoring to gain the favor of her employers.

In fact, Zita's employers were often angry with her because she could not resist giving so much food away. One of the miracles for which she was sainted occurred when she was leaving the Fatinelli house with her apron full of bread scraps. A member of the family caught her and demanded to see what she was concealing. When Zita opened her apron, the bread had been miraculously turned into flowers. Today Catholics honor Zita as the patron saint of servant girls.

of Winchester. Scholar Michael Adler says, "Her direct relations with the king and the Court, her extensive and successful transactions, her co-operation with the principal Jewish banker of the day—all mark her as an outstanding personality."[37] Lending to the rich and powerful was not without its risks for Licoricia, including imprisonment until certain taxes were paid and under a false accusation of theft, and the requirement that she make a large charitable donation to a cause favored by the king. Baskin writes:

"She was twice imprisoned on charges that were later dismissed and made large contributions towards the building of Westminster Abbey. Her five sons, who described themselves as 'sons of Licoricia,' also became moneylenders, continuing their mother's business after her murder in 1277."[38]

Businesswomen of Great Wealth

A few medieval businesswomen were so successful that they accumulated very large fortunes. Shulamith Shahar relates the story of one, Rose Burford, who inherited great wealth from her husband but increased it due to her own energetic and effective business management:

Rose Burford, widow of a rich merchant who loaned a large sum to the king to finance his Scottish wars in 1318, continued her husband's business after his death. When the debt due to her husband was not repaid even after she submitted several petitions, she proposed to the king that it be repaid in the form of exemption from the tax she was due to pay for wool she wished to export. She was summoned to court to submit her plea, the proposal was examined and her request was granted.[39]

Marty Williams and Anne Echols discuss several other medieval women with businesses of significant size. "Alice Horsford was half-owner of a vessel, the *Saynte Mariebot,* which was based in London in 1370. As a 'sleeping partner,' she received some of the merchandise or profits after each trip."[40] Other woman merchants include Mabilia Lecavella, who sold wine to the king of France in the early 1200s, and Joanna Rowley, who in 1479 imported sugar from Lisbon, Portugal, and sold it in Spain and England. The importer Margery Russell appears in the court records because Spanish pirates had seized some of her ships, which she valued at eight hundred pounds. By petitioning the court, Margery obtained letters of marque, which gave her the king's permission to seize two Spanish ships in compensation for her loss.

One of the boldest and most successful medieval businesswomen of all, Gertrude Morneweg, lived in the frontier city of Lubeck (in the northeast of what is now Germany). She was the widow of a wealthy merchant, and after his death in 1286 she administered these enterprises with great skill, withdrawing from the import-export business and making investments within the city of Lubeck. In fact, her investments were essential to the city's economy. As historian Edith Ennen explains:

> At that time Lubeck had overstretched itself in buying [rights to] the River Wahenitz; its water was needed for the mills that ground the flour for export to Norway and Sweden. Widow Morneweg made large credits available to the town, and also financed a number of respected old families who owned valuable properties that were used as security for the credit. Some quickly repaid their debt, but others sank into a financial dependence which led to the loss of their properties. By 1301, Gertrude Morneweg had invested about 14,500 Lubeck marks in bonds, a sum worth millions of marks in modern purchasing power.[41]

The Dignity of Work

A few medieval women owned ships or could afford to finance the wars of kings and the bond markets of entire cities.

A medieval woman hangs laundry, just one of the many jobs occupied by women.

Thousands of other women participated in skilled crafts and filled occupations essential to the economies of the cities and towns where they lived. Nevertheless, it is important to remember that in the Middle Ages, most women had few choices in life and work. In fact, as Goldberg argues,

> Very real limitations . . . circumscribed their lives. From many aspects of medieval life women were deliberately excluded. As a consequence, many retreated to the margins of the urban

economy as hucksters, second-hand clothes dealers and petty traders, positions tolerated by civic authorities without enthusiasm. [42]

Women could be members of some craft guilds, but with only a few exceptions they had no voice in guild affairs. Some medieval men could buy the right to own a retail store in a city, but few women had enough money to do this. In York, for example, between 1272 and 1500 only 147 women purchased the right to own a shop; this is only 1 percent of the total for all of those years.

Indeed, as work became increasingly industrialized and the Middle Ages merged into the modern era, it became more and more difficult for women to support themselves independently outside of marriage.

Yet the achievements of the women who lived in the towns and cities of medieval Europe reflect their determination, enterprise, and creativity. As David Herlihy concludes:

"Work for all people is at once a duty and a dignity. Women fulfilled many jobs throughout the long medieval centuries. It is instructive, perhaps even inspiring, to survey the work that medieval women performed and the dignity that they earned." [43]

Chapter 3:
Women in the Professions

In the Middle Ages, women played significant roles in professions that, according to medieval theory, law, and custom, were reserved for men. As healers, some women were trained and licensed physicians. Others were nurses, midwives, and pharmacists, while a few founded hospitals or provided training for nurses. In contrast, no medieval woman was able to obtain formal training as a lawyer. Nevertheless, many women played the role of advocate and used the courts to defend their own rights and those of their husbands and families. Some medieval women even presided over courts and dispensed justice to others.

Medieval Health Care Practices

Medieval people took two approaches to medicine and health care, one focusing on theoretical scholarship and one devoted to practical applications. Theoretical knowledge, which was based on the writings of ancient authors such as Galen and Hippocrates, was taught in the universities and was known as "medicine." According to medieval medical theory, illness results from an "imbalance" of the "humors" in the body. Typically, a university-trained male physician, usually bearing the title "physician" or "master," would diagnose the illness by examining the patient's urine and would then prescribe a medication—often to be made from strange and expensive ingredients—to restore the proper balance between hot and cold, and wet and dry humors in the patient's body.

Most medieval healers, however, had no formal education. Their training was based on observation and experience with folk remedies. These low-prestige healers, who included most of the women, were known as "surgeons" and provided practical, hands-on treatment. The work of medieval surgeons merged into the services provided by barbers. Their training and practices had little in common with those of medieval physicians.

Surgeons and Barbers

Surgeons and barbers were practical healers who did far more than simply cutting hair. As scholar Carole Rawcliffe explains:

"Look Carefully"

In the Middle Ages, male physicians often diagnosed disease by inspecting a glass vial of urine, sometimes making no direct examination at all of the patient. Trotula's advice, in her book *The Diseases of Women*, is much closer to what a modern doctor would do to diagnose a patient's illness. The passage is taken from Elizabeth Brooke's *Women Healers Through History*.

A medieval patient places a vial of urine in the hands of a physician.

When you reach the patient, ask where his pain is, then feel his pulse. Touch his skin to see if he has a fever, ask if he has a chill, and when the pain began, and if it is worse at night. Watch his facial expression, test the softness of his abdomen, and ask if he passes urine frequently. Look carefully at the urine, examine his body for sensitive spots and if you find nothing ask what other doctors he has consulted and what was their diagnosis. Ask if he had ever had a similar attack and when. Then having found the cause of his trouble it will be easy to determine his treatment.

"The extraction of teeth, the manipulation of dislocated limbs, the lancing of boils and general treatment of scalds, burns and disfiguring skin diseases, the setting of bones and the suturing of wounds all fell to the surgeon's lot." [44]

Women were members of some European barbers' and surgeons' guilds. One such healer was "Katherine *la surgiene* of London, daughter of Thomas the Surgeon, and sister of William the Surgeon." [45] In 1286, accounting records show that the monks of Westminster Abbey employed both male and female surgeons (but paid the women less). In his will, Nicholas Bradmore, a surgeon in London, left his apprentice Agnes Woodcock a red belt with a silver buckle and six shillings and eight pence. Women have also been recorded as members of barbers' guilds in Lincoln and Norwich, England, and Dublin, Ireland.

Women Physicians

In the Middle Ages, barriers to gaining a university education prevented almost all women from receiving the formal credentials required to be known by the title of *medica, magistra, physica,* or *fisica* (the feminine forms of the Latin words for doctor, master, and physician). One important barrier was that girls were almost never taught Latin, the language used in medieval universities. Yet some women did become credentialed physi-cians. Joseph Shatzmiller, a scholar of medieval Jewish history, relates several instances from Manosque, a small city in Provence, France, as well as from other areas of Europe:

A document of May 1292, which probably contained the names of all the active doctors in Manosque, listed

Two women nurse an elderly man on his sickbed in this 1470 illustration.

a Christian woman named Laura de Digna among the 8 practitioners. A Jewess named Hava (or Hana) appears in a document in the early 1320s in her medical capacity. The Manosque Jewess Maryona, widowed in 1341, appears from 1342 in over forty documents, invariably and consistently styled *physica*. In fact, 3 other female doctors can be found among the 40 practitioners in Manosque in the mid–fourteenth century. To these women who practiced in one small city in Upper Provence can be added the names of dozens of other women, many of them Jewish, who practiced openly and officially in Spain, Italy, Germany, and elsewhere in Provence. [46]

A few other European women achieved recognition for their medical expertise. One was Hersende, a French woman doctor who was appointed by King Louis IX to be the "mistress physician" of the Seventh Crusade. Hersende oversaw the provision of medical and surgical services to the soldiers and camp followers and also assisted the queen in giving birth while on crusade in Egypt. According to Echols and Williams, "She received a life pension for her services, probably settled in Paris around 1250 and married Jacques, the royal apothecary." [47] Another European woman, Calenda Cost-anza, of Italy, became an academic physician and presented lectures on medicine in 1423. Also in the fifteenth century, sixteen women doctors are known to have practiced in the German trade center of Frankfurt am Main.

One of the few places where medieval women could receive formal training in medicine was Salerno, a city in the south of Italy. The medical school there was the oldest and most prestigious in Europe. To explain the power of Salerno's reputation throughout Europe, Herlihy relates this story about a woman poisoner from Normandy, in northern France:

> In 1085, Sichelgaita, wife of the Norman duke Robert Guiscard, tried to poison her brother-in-law Bohemond. She had been trained in poisons by the doctors of Salerno, who looked upon her as their *alumna,* or student. The plot failed, and Sichelgaita even had to provide an antidote for the sickened Bohemond. But Bohemond remained pale and feeble for the rest of his life. [48]

Trotula and *The Diseases of Women*

Of all the graduates of the medical school in Salerno, the most famous was a woman named Trotula, who became the best known of all medieval women physicians. Trotula's twelfth-century medical text-

Medical Advice from Trotula on the Care of Newborns

Although she was a trained physician, Trotula also gives commonsense advice in her medical textbook, *The Diseases of Women.* This section, translated in Elizabeth Brooke's *Women Healers Through History,* offers advice to the nurse, or caregiver, of a newborn:

> Let there be in front of him varied pictures, cloths of various colors, and pearls. In his presence one should employ songs and gentle voices and no one should sing with a harsh voice. Nor should there be noisy persons about. When the time for the baby to talk has come, the nurse should frequently anoint his tongue with honey and butter.... Frequent and gentle words should be spoken in front of him.... When the time shall come when he begins to eat, [a piece of bread the shape of a finger] should be given the infant. He can hold it in his hand and play with it, and sucking from it he will swallow some of it.

book, *The Diseases of Women,* was an important reference throughout Europe for hundreds of years, and its author is even mentioned in the greatest literary work of the Middle Ages, Chaucer's *Canterbury Tales.* One of Chaucer's characters, the Wife of Bath, tells her companions on pilgrimage that her husband likes to read excerpts from Trotula's works. Monica H. Green, a scholar who edited *The Diseases of Women* for modern readers, explains that it is "one of the pillars on which later medieval culture was built, being present in the libraries of physicians and surgeons, monks and philosophers, theologians and princes from Italy to Ireland, from Spain to Poland."[49]

Medical historian Elizabeth Brooke gives another illustration of Trotula's fame. In this story, a minstrel hopes to sell potions to a crowd of people at a fair. The fact that he uses Trotula's name to back up his sales pitch shows how famous she became:

> Good people, I am hardly one of your itinerant preachers, one of those raggle-taggle herbalists ... who carry boxes and sachets and spread them out on a carpet. No, I am a disciple of the great lady named Trotula of Salerno, who performs such marvels of every kind. And know ye she is the wisest woman in the four corners of the world.[50]

According to Elizabeth Brooke, Trotula's book shows "the gentle hand of the woman doctor on every page":

Trotula's first consideration when encountering a sick person was his or her comfort. She believed in treating patients gently, giving them medicated baths and suitable diets. Fires were to be lit if the house was cold and damp. Patients' faces were sprinkled with sweet-smelling extracts. For example, Trotula recommends oil of roses for foul-smelling ulcers. She believed in long convalescences; above all, whenever possible, she gave a hopeful prognosis. [51]

Apothecaries and Herbalists

In the Middle Ages, there were few pharmacies where people could purchase drugs, ointments, and other medical products already prepared for use. Instead, women commonly grew their own medicinal herbs and prepared their own potions and remedies as needed. In addition, some individual pharmacists, known as apothecaries, mixed and sold medicines; many of these were women.

Hildegard of Bingen, a German abbess who lived from 1098 to 1179, was very learned in the use of herbs and cured many illnesses using her skills as an apothecary. Hildegard wrote books on a wide variety of topics—more than any other woman of her time. One of the best-known is *Physica,* which, according to Herlihy, "describes the characteristics of humans, animals, fish, plants, and metals. She is especially remarkable for her knowledge of herbs; in her works she describes some 485 herbs and plants." [52]

Elizabeth Brooke quotes two passages from Hildegard's *Physica* that illustrate her extensive knowledge of herbal medicine. The first, on an herb called Dornella or tormentil, reflects the medieval theory that all natural things are either "hot" or "cold," with related medical effects:

Dornella (tormentil) is cold, and that coldness is good and healthy and useful against fevers that arise from bad food. Take tormentil therefore, and cook it in wine with a little honey added . . . and drink it fasting at night and you will be cured of the fever.

If any baby lying in its cradle is suffused and vexed with blood between the skin and flesh so that it is greatly troubled, take new and recent leaves from the aspen and put them in a simple linen cloth and wrap the baby in the leaves and cloth and put him down to sleep, wrapping him up so he will sweat and extract the virtue from the leaves, and he will get well. [53]

A medieval apothecary collects herbs for use in potions.

Women Healers

Medieval women in general were usually responsible for providing basic health care to their families. Some women drew on these practical skills to care for others as well, occasionally achieving enough success to arouse the jealousy and opposition of male doctors. A Parisian woman, Jacoba Félicie, achieved great success as an unlicensed healer—until she was brought to trial before the church authorities in 1322. The transcript of the case reveals much about Jacoba's skills and her distinctive approach to healing.

Jacoba visited the sick, examined them, and said, "I will cure you by God's will, if you will have faith in me."[54] Her agreement with the patient stated that she would receive a fee only if the patient recovered. Her remedies included syrups, potions, laxatives, digestives, and aromatics. One well-known patient was a monk named Dominus Odo de Cornessiaco. Jacoba stayed by his side, gave him massages with hot oil, steam baths, and poultices made from healing plants. She worked tirelessly until he was cured.

Jacoba also specialized in healing services for women. Medieval attitudes concerning modesty made it difficult for men to treat many women's illnesses. As Jacoba explained at her trial:

> It is better and more seemly that a wise woman learned in the art should visit the sick woman and inquire into the secrets of her nature and her hidden parts, than that a man should do so, for whom it is not lawful to see and seek out the aforesaid parts, nor to feel with his hands, the breasts, belly and feet of women. And a woman before now would allow herself to die, rather than reveal the secrets of her infirmities to a man.[55]

Many witnesses testified that Jacoba had cured them after male physicians, called "masters" in the transcript of the trial, had failed. Yet the judges in the church court did not believe this testimony, saying: "Her plea that she cured many sick persons whom the aforesaid masters could not cure, ought not to stand and is frivolous, since it is certain that a man approved in the aforesaid art [medicine] could cure the sick better than any woman."[56]

Generally the authorities, and especially the male physicians, were hostile to women healers. Shahar lists the names of a group of women who were fined for practicing medicine without a permit: "Clarice de Rotmago, a married woman; Johanna the convert [probably a Jewish physician who converted to Christianity]; Marguerite of Ypres, the surgeon; and Belota the Jewess."[57]

In England, Joanna Lee petitioned King Henry IV to be allowed to practice medicine after her husband's death on the king's service; her petition was denied. In Valencia, Spain, in 1329, a law was passed that said, "No woman may practice medicine or give potions, under penalty of being whipped through the town; but they may care for little children and women, to whom, however, they may give no potions."[58]

A thirteenth-century Icelandic saga shows a more positive attitude toward women healers. It describes the women of the Sturlunga family, who had important health care roles to play, given the violent culture of that country: They bandaged

A 1434 portrait honors a medieval woman who founded a hospital in Beaune, France.

wounds, built hospitals, and healed the sick. In one story, "a woman, Svanhvit [Swanwhite], finds her husband wounded in battle; she sews up his wounds and sends him back healed to fight again."[59]

Founders of Hospitals and Nursing Orders

A few medieval women established health care services that reached large groups of people. In 1126, Bertha, sister-in-law of Anna Comnena of Constantinople (now Istanbul, Turkey), built a large hospital called the Pantocrator to house wounded pilgrims. Each of its five sections was run by a woman doctor, and the work was divided between midwives, male and female nurses, and surgeons. At one time the hospital was run by an Englishwoman, Edina Rittle of Essex.

Eleanor of Aquitaine, queen of first France and then England, built hospitals along the paths of the Crusades. Her daughter Isobel founded the nursing order of the Poor Clares, who devoted their lives to the sick and the dying. They grew their own medicinal plants and had their own pharmacies. Isobel's granddaughter Hedwig, queen of Silesia, Poland, and Slavic Croatia, "built hospitals, tended the sick in clinics, and had feeding programs for the hungry and destitute. She and her family built over 18,000 asylums for lepers in her

A medieval manuscript page portrays a scene from a fourteenth-century hospital.

realm,"[60] according to Brooke. Hedwig's niece, St. Elizabeth of Hungary, who was born in 1207, trained women in nursing, binding wounds, soothing fevers, and easing pain.

Midwives

Medieval midwives played a role between that of today's obstetrician and that of a labor room nurse, assisting women in giving birth. In the Middle Ages, women also asked midwives for help in becoming pregnant, and in predicting the sex of their unborn child. Babies were born in the mother's home, whether a one-room cottage or a castle. During labor, the midwife calmed the mother, often bathing her with sweet-scented water, feeding her broth, and rubbing ointment into her skin.

Many midwives had high-level medical skills—for example, the ability to turn a baby while in the birth canal so that it could be born headfirst, avoiding a dangerous breech birth. In general, midwives were responsible for delivering live or stillborn infants, sometimes performing a cesarean section (a surgical operation) to do so, and for stopping excessive bleeding after a birth.

These services were so valued that wealthy women occasionally remembered their midwives in their wills. For example, Margery Cobbe of Devon, England, attended Elizabeth, wife of King Edward IV, as she gave birth. In gratitude, Elizabeth left Margery a pension of ten pounds per year.

Women Advocates in Manorial Courts

A manorial court was a rural institution that helped the lord of the manor exercise control over the village and its people, while also filling the villagers' need for regulation of the community in which they lived. Held every three weeks, these courts dealt with even the most minor of matters, and all landholders were required to attend. Judith Bennett explains:

> Most contacts in medieval courts involved cooperation and exchange rather than controversy and enmity. And the professional expertise that so dominates modern courts was minimized in manorial courts; the lord or his representative presided over the proceedings and provided a clerk to keep the record, but business was conducted by lay-people who usually acted without the aid of lawyers or other counselors.[61]

Although no medieval women were formally trained as lawyers, they did appear frequently in court, defending and representing themselves as well as their husbands and families. A few medieval women even presided over manorial courts and handed down judicial decisions to those who appeared before them. According to Herlihy:

Noble women continued to inherit offices which empowered them to serve as judges or advocates. . . . On the religious level, the faithful were instructed to address the Virgin Mary as *advocata,* the gracious advocate of sinners before the court of heaven. Finally, in all courts women were allowed to speak in their own defense. [62]

Though women lacked the standing to represent themselves or to argue against a man according to custom and law in the Middle Ages, records show that women often were successful advocates for their own interests. As Williams and Echols point out:

Obviously legal theory and practice rarely coincided. Though females had no legal standing as adults, women actually appeared at court in a variety of roles. In fourteenth-century Ghent [now in Belgium], Callekin van Luerne even went to court to argue her right to protect herself. The jurors decided that she had been justified in wounding a male assailant with a knife. [63]

In Brigstock, England, the widow Alice Avice made extensive use of the manorial court to protect her rights to her land, which was the most valuable asset in medieval times:

A fourteenth-century painting shows an adulterous wife (left with scroll) as she defends herself in court.

Usually coming to court unaccompanied by others, she paid rent on her holding, she purchased and sold lands, she answered for various offenses associated with property ownership, she brought or responded to six complaints against other villagers, and she even acted on three occasions as a legal surety, guaranteeing that others would meet their legal obligations. [64]

Representing a Husband or Family in Court

In theory, a married woman was under the protection and control of her husband.

Yet some medieval husbands relied on their wives to represent their interests in court. For example, Williams and Echols write that in 1280, John Gardebois of London "appointed his wife, Avice, as his attorney and charged her with collecting his debts."[65] A century later, another woman, Clare van der Ponten of Ghent, had legal responsibility for her husband's business, which involved buying and selling wool and land.

Goldberg discusses a group of English noblewomen who used the courts actively to collect debts owed to their families or to preserve their rights to land:

> Between 1473 and 1476 Anne Neville, dowager duchess of Buckingham had suits pending against twenty-three people for recovery of debts and Lady Margaret Beaufort, as guardian of Edward, duke of Buckingham, brought twenty-eight suits for debt on her ward's estates in 1437–8, just before he came of age. Of Margaret Beaufort it can fairly be said that an acute sense of her legal rights and pursuit of her dues by legal means was one of the keys to her highly successful administration.[66]

Women Who Dispensed Justice

A few women of the landowning classes, especially those who were widowed or whose husbands were absent, administered their own courts. For fifty years Ermengarde, who was a viscountess in the south of France in the twelfth century, dispensed justice throughout the manors of her large estates. According to Williams and Echols, she "was famous for her judgments in difficult legal proceedings."[67] Another French noblewoman,

> Lady Eustacia of Brou, the wife of William Gouet II . . . joined with him in hearing matters brought to their court. . . . During her husband's absence on crusade, Eustacia frequently held court and dispensed justice. Her two grown sons witnessed her acts but did not attempt to usurp their mother's authority as feudal lord. When William returned around 1115 he found the family fiefs in good shape and order maintained. Countess Adela of Blois, Chartres, and Meaux, who was a contemporary of Eustacia, also acted with her husband, Count Stephen, in determining and administering justice and she, too, assumed control of these counties while he was on crusade. Count Stephen, however, died in the East, and Adela remained in control of these counties for well over a decade.[68]

Williams and Echols add, "Similarly, during her husband's absence, Margaret

Paston convened her own fifteenth-century manorial courts to hear complaints and arbitrate disputes among local villagers." Another Englishwoman, Angareta de Beauchamp, owned a manor called Spelsburg; in addition, she "owned the right to convene courts and operate her own gallows. . . . These privileges were very profitable because courts garnered fines and confiscated property."[69]

Countless medieval women served their families, their communities, and their personal interests as healers or advocates. Some achieved the highest level of professional training or became famous for their writing. Others are known today only through court or business records. In all cases these medieval women set the stage for the work of the professional healers and advocates who would follow them in the modern era.

Chapter 4:
Women Estate Administrators

❧

Medieval women of property—from the nobility to the landed gentry—played a vital role in administering estates. Many began this work as teenage brides, continued to carry out significant managerial responsibilities during their marriages, and later defended their own and their families' interests as widows. Administering an estate required skill, confidence, and determination in supervising and providing for a household that could number in the hundreds and could move between castles on a monthly basis. Sometimes courage was also a necessity—when defending a manor house or castle from military attack. Women administrators were also responsible for politicking to maintain and advance the welfare of the family, for providing military leadership, and for managing the profitability and finances of far-flung estates.

The Landowner Household

The noble household could be very large—some included as many as four hun-dred people—and managing it required a high level of administrative skill and personal leadership. Even gentry households could move frequently between several manors and be composed of dozens of servants and many family members. Historian Jennifer C. Ward explains that these challenges

> applied to any noble household, whether headed by a lord or a lady. It is, however, important to stress the number of households in the later Middle Ages under the control of women on a temporary or permanent basis, during absences of husbands, or during widowhood. These women had an important part to play in the context of noble and gentry society; through their use of hospitality, the exchange of gifts, and the development of social contacts, they exercised influence on behalf of their families, households and the communities around them. [70]

The Paston Letters and Account Rolls of Noble Households

Some of the remarkable women who administered estates are known today through the detailed documents created for them by their staffs. Notable among these records are letters dictated in the fifteenth century by the women of the Paston family, especially Margaret Paston. The Paston letters are practical documents that deal with family issues, lawsuits, and administration of the Pastons' manors in East Anglia, England. The family placed a very high value on their letters and carefully preserved them as a record of their affairs. As Margaret wrote to her oldest son,

> Keep wisely your writings that are of charge [important], that they come not into the hands of those that may hurt you hereafter. Your father, whom God assoil [pardon], in his

---

In the Castle Kitchen

❧

Marty Williams and Anne Echols, in *Women in the Middle Ages,* used the household account rolls of an English noblewoman, Dame Alice de Bryene, to illustrate the challenge of providing one day's meals for a large medieval household and its frequent guests:

> On an average day—Thursday, August 17, 1413, for example—Dame Alice de Bryene served one hundred and forty-six loaves of bread, one and a half quarters of beef, a lamb, two mutton joints, three quarters of bacon, and thirty pigeons, all washed down with ale and wine. . . . Alice de Bryene's household accounts show that on most days her kitchens provided for her large household, several guests, and a number of boon workers—villains engaged in performing their required days of extra work on their lord's demesne (the lord's portion of the manor lands).

Musicians play for a medieval family at dinner.

---

troubled season set more [store] by his writings and evidence than he did by any of his moveable goods. Remember that if they were taken from you, you could never get any more such as they are. [71]

Also surviving are rolls of parchment containing several noblewomen's household accounts. These were compiled for each day and then summarized yearly. Ward explains, "Individual departments of the household produced their own accounts for incorporation in the yearly roll, particular members of the household, such as children, were accounted for separately, and separate accounting is also found for journeys." [72]

Among the households whose accounts have survived is that of Eleanor de Montfort, sister of King Henry III, who was already a widow when she married Simon de Montfort at age sixteen. Marty Williams and Anne Echols write that the wife of a landowner:

directed the officials who ran the large staff of servants, entertained a variety of people, controlled estate finances, provided for adequate supplies, and commanded the defense of her home. In the spring and summer of 1265, Eleanor de Montfort, countess of Leicester, competently performed all these tasks. In addition, she kept in constant touch with her husband and sons while moving her household from castle to castle in preparation for war—another common duty for a nobleman's wife. [73]

Supervising the Household

Regardless of the challenges of frequent travel and preparations for war, a landowner's wife had to make sure that the entire household was clothed and fed throughout the year. She was also responsible for managing the work of the servants and laborers who produced much of the food and cloth needed by the household. As Williams and Echols describe the roles played by the noble or gentry woman:

She had to be an able administrator and organizer, as well as a tactful labor negotiator. She might purchase some fabric, but she usually also had to supervise home clothmaking—carding, spinning, weaving, and sewing. If she lived on a rural estate, the huge job of seeing to the provisions for the entire household might also fall on her shoulders. Since only cities had well-stocked marketplaces, this task involved acquiring, monitoring, and storing supplies well in advance of demand. Her provisioning duties would include supervising the following tasks: caring for the livestock, smoking meats, baking, brewing, cheese- and butter-making,

A fourteenth-century manuscript page shows an upper-class, landowning family. Often the wives were responsible for the daily functions of the household.

stocking provisions for the winter, and tending to the kitchen garden.[74]

A letter written in October 1448 shows how Margaret Paston strove to provide the food and military supplies needed in one of the family manors, called Gresham, "a square, fortified, and moated manor house with towers at the corners." She wrote to John to send crossbows and arrows "for your house here is so low that there may no man shoot out with a long bow. . . . And also I would that you should get two or three short poleaxes . . . and as many jacks [body armor] as you may." Margaret's letter gives the news of another manor being fortified against the duke of Suffolk's men, and then lists the goods that she needs her husband to buy in London:

I pray that you will vouchsafe to order for me one pound of almonds

Keeping the Money Safe

Margaret Paston took responsibility for counting what she calls "your money" in letters to her husband. This letter to John (quoted in Frances and Joseph Gies, *A Medieval Family: The Pastons of Fifteenth-Century England*), shows some of the measures that Margaret took to protect her family's wealth:

> I have taken measure in the drawing room chamber, where you want your coffers and desk to be set. . . . There is no space beside the bed, even if

the bed is removed to the door, to set both your board [a medieval counting device somewhat like an abacus] and your coffers there, and to have room to go and sit beside it. Wherefore I have purveyed that you shall have the same drawing chamber that you had before there, where you shall lie by yourself; and when your gear is moved out of your little house, the door shall be locked, and your bags laid in one of the great coffers, so that they shall be safe, I trust.

and one pound of sugar, and that you will order some frieze [woolen cloth] to make your children's gowns. You shall have the best price and best choice from Hayes's wife, as it is told me. And that you would buy a yard of broadcloth of black and a hood for me, of 44 pence or 4 shillings a yard, for there is neither good cloth nor good frieze in this town.[75]

Financial Administration

Maintaining a noble or gentry household was very costly. For this reason it was important that the medieval woman landowner not neglect her responsibility for collecting fees from tenants who paid a flat sum called a "farm" to raise crops on her land. She also had to be sure that her officials gathered in the rents from her peasants, both in cash and in the form of produce. If she received produce, as Margaret Paston did from some of her family's tenants, the landowner had to see that it was sold profitably or processed and stored for later use. It is clear from various letters that the Pastons regularly sold wool and malt that had been produced on their manors.

About 1460, Margaret wrote to John to report on the financial health of the Paston estates, including a manor called Hellesden. As Frances and Joseph Gies summarize Margaret's words:

All his wool had been sold, at a good price. Three horses had been bought for him at St. Faith's Fair, "and all be trotters, right fair horses." His mills at Hellesden had been leased for 12 marks, the miller to pay for their repair "and Richard Calle [the Pastons' bailiff] has let all your lands at Caister" [a castle inherited from Sir John Fastolf].[76]

Marriage Among Landholders

Marriage often plunged a young woman into a role as an estate manager, and arranging marriages that would be beneficial to the noble family was also a duty many mothers had to take on. Marriages among landholders were always arranged to preserve or, it was hoped, increase the value of the family estates. Not only did an heiress add her land to her husband's, but she then assumed considerable responsibility for administering both of the properties and making them profitable. According to historian Amy Livingstone,

> After marriage a woman would most likely move into her husband's place of residence where she would assume responsibility for overseeing the estates of her husband and keeping track of the revenue and income generated by these properties. One can imagine that a new bride charged with con-

siderable responsibilities was thankful for the lessons on budgets and household finance instilled by her mother.[77]

Margaret Mautby was an heiress, and her manors were close to those of the Paston family. For that reason she was a very desirable match for John Paston. After their first meeting at Reedham, which was one of Margaret's family's manors, John's mother, Agnes Paston, wrote this letter to her husband, William, about the marriage negotiations:

A noble couple, joined in marriage, walk together in their wedding procession.

Blessed be God I send you good tidings of the coming, and the bringing home, of the gentlewoman that you know of from Reedham this same night....And as for the first acquaintance between John Paston and the said gentlewoman, she made him gentle cheer in gentle wise, and said he was truly your son. And so I hope there shall need no great treaty [marriage negotiation] between them. The parson of Stockton told me if you would buy her a gown, her mother would give thereto a goodly fur. The gown needs to be bought; and of color it would be a goodly blue, or else a bright sanguine [red]. [78]

John and Margaret married about 1440, and Margaret's property, which was worth about 150 pounds per year, was then added to the Paston estates. Their marriage appears to have been a happy one, producing at least eight children, including daughters Anne and Margery, of whom seven survived into adulthood. Margaret died about 1484, when she was about sixty-four years of age.

Landholding in Times of War

In times of war noble families faced particular challenges. Noblemen held their land in return for military service that enabled their king to retain or achieve domination over lands both near and far. For this rea-son, noblemen often had to travel to foreign countries to fight a war or go on a crusade. During the Hundred Years' War, an intermittent conflict between England and France lasting from 1337 to 1453, noblemen frequently had to fight either in distant battles or in defense of their own landholdings. In addition, noble families had to contribute increasing amounts of tax as the kings involved in the war struggled to finance their campaigns.

Political instability was another source of problems. King Henry VI of England experienced extended periods of mental illness; as a result, the central government was weak. Many English lords tried to seize power and land within England. This period, known as the Wars of the Roses—from the symbols of the two main factions, the white rose of the Yorkists and the red rose of the Lancastrians—caused severe hardships for peasants, landholders, and the wives or widows who were administering English estates. At this time, Margaret Paston had to deal with constant harassment and attacks on the family manors by the duke of Suffolk. Frances and Joseph Gies write that this nobleman, "whose position in the national government was approximately that of prime minister, tyrannized East Anglia through . . . lawyers, local office-holders and bullies who threatened, robbed, and extorted from their fellow countrymen." [79]

Women of the Middle Ages

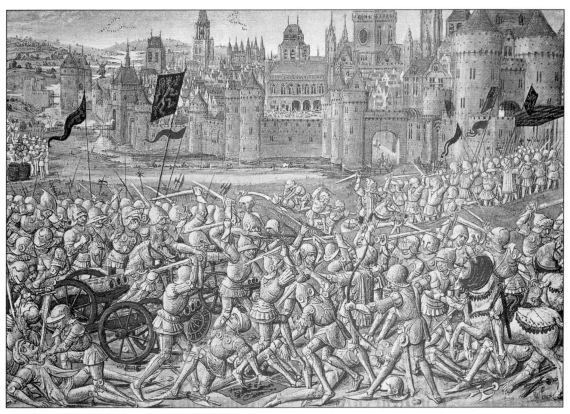

A medieval battlefield. Women had to be wise administrators during periods of war and unrest.

Absent Husbands

Attacks like these show how difficult for their wives the frequent absences of medieval husbands could be. These absences were especially challenging for wives who were still in their teens when they were left alone to administer a complex estate. Dame Alice de Bryene, for example, married in 1376 at age fourteen or fifteen. Ten years later—her husband having spent most of those years fighting in Europe—she was widowed and left to raise two daughters. Dame Alice had three manors to administer, amounting to six thousand acres of land in different parts of England. Medieval writer Christine de Pizan referred to challenges like these when she wrote: "Because barons and still more commonly knights and squires and gentlemen travel and go off to the wars, their wives should be wise and sound administrators and manage their affairs well, because most of the time they stay at home without their husbands, who are at court or abroad."[80]

The fortunes—or misfortunes—of war could place additional demands on wives beyond simply those caused by the absence

Manual for His Wife

A wealthy Frenchman, known today only as "The Householder of Paris," wrote a manual to instruct his young wife in the duties she would assume upon her marriage to him (quoted in Emilie Amt, ed., *Women's Lives in Medieval Europe: A Sourcebook*). The householder expected his wife to play many different and demanding roles. This family lived in a house in the city but also managed an estate in the countryside. The manual, written about 1392, is divided into sections, and then into "articles":

The first article is that you take care of your household with diligence and perseverance and respect for work; take pains to find pleasure therein and I will do likewise on my part. . . .

The second article is that at the least you take pleasure and have some little skill in the care and cultivation of a garden, grafting in due season and keeping roses in winter.

The third article is that you know how to choose manservants, doorkeepers, handymen or other strong folk to perform the heavy work that from hour to hour must be done, and likewise laborers, etc. And also tailors, shoemakers, bakers, pastrymakers, etc. And in particular how to set the household manservants and chambermaids to work, to sift

and winnow grain, clean dresses, air and dry, and how to order your folk to take thought for the sheep and horses and keep and amend wines.

The fourth article is that you, as sovereign mistress of your house, know how to order dinners, suppers, dishes and courses, and be wise in that which concerns the butcher and the poulterer, and have knowledge of spices.

The fifth article is that you know how to order, ordain, devise and have made all manner of pottages [soups], civeys [relishes], sauces and all other meats, and the same for sick folk.

The third section tells of games and amusements that are pleasant enough to keep you in countenance and give you something to talk about in company, and contains three articles.

The first article is concerned with amusing questions, which are set out and answered in strange fashion by the chance of dice and by rooks and kings.

The second article is how to feed and fly the falcon.

The third article tells of certain other riddles concerning counting and numbering, which are subtle to find out and guess.

of the lord from the estate. Rowena Archer writes,

> Katherine Neville, married in 1412, had charge of the vast Mobray estates from 1417 to 1422 when her husband, John, served an unbroken period in France for Henry V. . . . Imprisonment as a result of war brought wives the extra burden of raising a ransom, while incarceration for crime or political miscalculation brought, in addition to administrative pressure, an immeasurable degree of painful ignominy [dishonor] and uncertainty.[81]

Political Responsibilities

Women of the gentry and nobility made great efforts to maintain their families' standing in the community and to keep good relations with neighboring lords. It was important to present a powerful image, suitable to the family's standing. The scholar ffiona Swabey explains:

> The hospitality of the household, providing meals for neighbors, friends, workers and occasional strangers, was an essential and fundamental part of medieval social behavior. For kings, bishops, lords and ladies the household was also a political powerbase and hospitality was not merely a domestic affair. It was a means of dispensing patronage and reminding neighbors of the social hierarchy.[82]

It was also essential to demonstrate the proper respect for those in power over the family. After the death of the Pastons' major patron, Sir John Fastolf, for example, Margaret wanted to be sure to observe proper mourning rituals. The period of mourning could affect even the tradition of playing games and putting on plays to celebrate Christmas. According to Frances and John Gies,

> She sent their eldest son to inquire of Lady Morely, a wealthy and noble widow, "what sports were used in her house on the Christmas following the decease of my Lord her husband." Lady Morely replied that "there were no disguisings [theatricals] nor harping, nor luting, nor singing, nor loud disports [games], but playing at the tables [backgammon], and chess and cards." Such games she gave her people leave to play and no other.[83]

Military Leadership

Military leadership could be important for a medieval landowner's wife, even if she were not a ruler or a warrior. She might still need to rally her servants and tenants in defense of the castle or manor house. Ward tells of two European noblewomen in this situation: Nicolaa de la Haye, who succeeded, and the countess of Buchan, who failed.

In the early thirteenth century, Nicolaa de la Haye defended the castle of Lincoln from French invaders. Defending castles and towns was a dangerous business and could have severe consequences if the defender was not successful. For most of his reign, King Edward I of England was at war with the Scots. The countess of Buchan attempted to defend Berwick Castle from the onslaught of the English. She, however, was not successful. To humiliate his vanquished enemy, Edward had the countess placed in a cage that was hung over the walls. [84]

In January 1449, retainers of the duke of Suffolk attacked the house where Margaret Paston was staying with her children and household, her husband being in London. John Paston made this petition to Parliament:

A riotous people to the number of a thousand persons arrayed in manner of war, with cuirasses [armor for the chest and back], bringandines [coats of mail], jacks [body armor], sallets [helmets], glaives [swords], bows, arrows, shields, guns, pans with fire . . . burning therein, long crooks to pull down the walls, and long trees with which they broke up gates and doors, and so came into the said mansion, the wife of your beseecher being at that time therein, and twelve persons with her; the which persons they drove out of the said mansion, and mined down the wall of the chamber wherein the wife of your said beseecher was, and bore her out at the gates, and cut asunder the posts of the houses and let them fall, and broke up all the chambers and coffers within the said mansion, and rifled them, and in the manner of robbery bore away all the stuff, array, and money that your said beseecher and his servants had there, to the value of £200, and part thereof sold, and part thereof given away, and the remainder they divided among them, to the great and outrageous hurt of your said beseecher. [85]

Even in this frightening and dangerous situation, John appears to take for granted that Margaret will deal with the aftermath. His letter to her does praise her but makes no promise to rush home and help: "I thank you for your labor and effort in dealing with the unruly fellowship that came before you last Monday, about which I have heard a report. And in good faith you acquitted yourself very well and discreetly and heartily, to your honor and mine, and to the shame of your adversaries."[86]

Later, the duke of Suffolk took possession of the city of Norwich and sent a large force of men to attack the Paston manor of Hellesden, which was only two miles outside the city. Margaret was not in residence at the time, but she rode there quickly to assess the damage and report back to John:

> In good faith, no creature can think how foully and horribly it is arrayed unless they see it. Many people come every day to wonder at it, both from Norwich and other places, and they speak of it with shame. The duke would have been better off by a thousand pounds if it had never been done, and you have the good will of the people because it is so foully done. The duke's men . . . put the parson out of the church til they had done, and ransacked every man's house in the town five or six times. . . . As for the lead, brass, pewter, iron, doors, gates, and other stuff of the houses, men from Costessy and Cawton have it, and what they could not carry away they have hewn asunder in the most malicious way. If it might be I wish some men of worship might be sent from the king to see how it is . . . before the snow falls, that they may make report of

A page from a medieval manuscript shows a woman as defender and heroine of the household.

the truth, or it shall not be seen so plain as now.[87]

Husbands' Respect for Their Wives' Abilities

Medieval documents sometimes reflect the high regard in which some women were held by their male relations. As Ward explains:

A medieval husband and his wife. Often a husband's reliance on his wife led to mutual respect in many medieval households.

The appointment of noblewomen to execute wills, and their increasingly favorable treatment over jointure and dower [two forms of landholding by women] indicate that husbands, fathers and brothers considered that they were quite capable of tackling business matters. Although abilities obviously varied, many widows in the later Middle Ages were vigorous and successful in furthering the fortunes of themselves and their families. [88]

Alice Chaucer was the granddaughter of the poet Geoffrey Chaucer, author of *The Canterbury Tales,* and the wife of the duke of Suffolk (the nobleman who held a high position in the national government, and who made so many attacks on the Pastons). The duke had so much respect for her that he made her the executrix of his will, explaining, "for above all the earth my singular trust is most in her." [89]

On March 29, 1098, Stephen, Count of Blois-Chartres, who was away from home on a crusade, wrote to his wife, Adela of Blois, "I strongly advise you to act firmly, to watch with care over my lands, to do your duty duly as it should be done to our children and vassals. You will see me as soon as I can return to you. Adieu." [90]

Resolute medieval women of the noble and gentry classes administered their estates effectively and forcefully. Their efforts preserved and often increased the value of their family lands. Many medieval wives deserved the praise of Christine de Pizan, who wrote, "Any man is extremely foolish, of whatever class he may happen to be, if he sees that he has a good and wise wife yet does not give her the authority to govern." [91]

Chapter 5:
Women in Power

Feudal rulers rarely felt secure. They sometimes faced the threat of invasion by those who wanted to seize their land, and more often they risked being outmaneuvered politically by family members or the lords and knights who were their vassals but hoped to supplant them. To hold onto their estates and the power that came with that land, lords had to be able warriors and astute rulers. Noblewomen were generally excluded from either role, as Christine Owans explains:

> Noblewomen were uniformly prohibited from performing the essential public duties required of each landholder by the king. They could not serve on juries, act as judges, or be summoned to court. Noblewomen could not become knights, join military organizations, or participate in any military aspect of medieval society.[92]

Yet some women, through a combination of circumstances and innate ability, became powerful warriors, influential leaders, and strong rulers. Some did this by stepping outside the conventional roles of wife (and mother) or nun. Others carved out positions of power within those conventional roles.

Pawns and Power Brokers

Despite their prestigious titles, queens and princesses of the Middle Ages were not necessarily powerful. While kings, dukes, and other noblemen had authority over soldiers and courts of law, their wives had little visible power and were expected to behave quite differently from men. Historian Derek Baker describes the distinction between queens and kings:

> One thing is clear ... the good queen was not seen to be active. While the good king led armies, pronounced judgements, and gave laws, the good queen was publicly pious, charitable, and managed her affairs through intermediaries, supervising without appearing to supervise.[93]

Indeed, because of their social position, noblewomen were often pawns in the power games of the men who controlled their lives. They were betrothed and married because the marriage created or completed an allegiance between lords or because the dowry a noblewoman brought

Eleanor of Aquitaine

Eleanor of Aquitaine was probably the most powerful woman of the medieval era. She inherited the dukedom of Aquitaine—a large and wealthy area in the west of today's France—when she was just fifteen, and then married a prince who soon became King Louis VII of France. She went with him on crusade, but became impatient with his personality and style of leadership. She persuaded church authorities to annul the marriage and went on to marry Henry, duke of Normandy, who was ten years younger than Eleanor.

Henry's ambition matched Eleanor's, and he soon set out for England, where he would claim the throne and become King Henry II. Eleanor administered their vast combined estates in France before joining him in England where they rode together from castle to castle reinforcing their rule.

Eleanor had two children with Louis and eight with Henry. She educated her children in statesmanship and arranged marriages for them to the key royalty and nobility of Europe. She became estranged from Henry and conspired with three of her sons to overthrow him, but the attempt failed, and Eleanor tried to escape by dressing as a knight. She was found out, and Henry imprisoned her.

When her son Richard I (known as Richard the Lion Heart) became king, Eleanor was active in his administration. He went on crusade, and she—at the age of seventy—made the long and arduous journey to Sicily to bring him the woman she had chosen to be his wife. On his return, Richard was captured and held for ransom, and Eleanor took charge. She strengthened Richard's castles against an expected attack by her son John, who had allied himself with Philip, son of her first husband, Louis. Then she raised the huge sum of money demanded for the ransom.

Eleanor remained active and powerful to the end of her life. At the age of eighty she was held hostage by her own grandson, but she got a message out to her son John, who rescued her. Her eventful life and dazzling personality inspired countless songs and poems.

The powerful and charismatic Eleanor of Aquitaine.

to her marriage included territory that was strategically important to her new husband. For example, Ermengarde de Beaumont was married to King William of Scotland in 1186 to fulfill the terms of a peace treaty. And the Irish nobleman Dermot McMurrough gave his daughter, Aoife, in marriage to Richard FitzGilbert de Clare (known as Strongbow) in 1170 in exchange for troops that would come to Ireland and help McMurrough crush his rival Tiernan O'Rourke.

However, some women were able to carve out positions of power for themselves, and others found themselves in a position in which they were called on to act as leaders. Many noblemen, when they went on crusade or to fight distant battles, left their estates in the hands of their wives. These women were in an unusual position, because they had some power (even though temporary) without having to break from their conventional role as wives. Indeed, it was because they were obedient wives that they were given and took on this responsibility. Some of these noblewomen showed considerable courage and leadership ability. Alice Knyvet was left in charge of the castle of Bokenham in England in 1461 and had to defend it from attack by the forces of King Edward IV. When the king sent a group of eleven officials to claim the castle, she defiantly declared, "I will not leave possession of this castle . . . and if you begin to break the peace or make war to get the place of me, I shall defend me." [94]

Widows Exercising Power

Jennifer C. Ward describes the circumstances that allowed—even obliged—some noblewomen to take up the reins of power:

A few noblewomen like Joan de Bohun, countess of Hereford and Essex, emerged as leading figures of their counties. Joan was widowed in 1373 and the Bohun inheritance was divided between her daughters who married . . . the duke of Gloucester . . . and Henry Bolingbroke, the future Henry IV. With the murder of the duke of Gloucester in 1397, and the accession of Henry IV two years later, and in the absence of other prominent nobles in Essex in the early fifteenth century, Joan was responsible . . . for quelling disorder and maintaining royal interests. [95]

Widows like Joan de Bohun were in a unique position in the medieval power structure. They often inherited their husband's land, or if the son who was to inherit was still young, the widow acted for him until he grew old enough to take power for himself. Christine Owens describes the influence widows could have:

Once widowed, a medieval noble-woman could elect to remain unmarried and many of those who did so took control of their property and their lives on a more permanent basis. These women ... were able to make important and lasting contributions to the political, economic, and social fabric of society by virtue of their highly visible position and their great wealth. [96]

In the early fourteenth century, Mahaut of Artois ruled her vast estates for twenty years after the death of her husband, Othon IV, count of Burgundy. She built up the economy of the region by promoting the cloth industry, and she supported hospitals and the arts.

Blanche of Navarre became countess of Champagne when she married Theobald, count of Champagne, in 1199. He died just two years later, leaving his estates to his infant son. Blanche acted as her son's regent until 1222, ruling for him. It was a time of political and military tumult in the region, and Blanche had to act resolutely and wisely to retain Champagne for her son. She was remarkably successful, and, as Echols and Williams record, "won the right to be direct vassal of [the] French king; and even attended a royal parliament in 1213." [97]

Some widowed queens and noble-women had a talent for leadership and used their years as regents—standing in

Widowed medieval women were in many cases able to maintain the power of their husbands.

for their young children—to build up a strong territory for the heir to inherit. Echols and Williams describe the life of Theresa, a countess of Portugal:

Her father married Theresa to Henry of Burgundy around 1095 with a dowry of Oporto and Coimbra. When Henry died around 1112, their son Alfonso Henriques was very young, so Theresa served as his regent. She continued Henry's policies—building an independent kingdom of Portugal. Unscrupulous and ambitious, Theresa was, nonetheless, a capable and courageous ruler. She led troops, encouraged urban growth, and instilled national feelings in the Portuguese.... Her son wrested control of Portugal from her in 1128, but it was Theresa's previous efforts which allowed Alfonso Henriques to become first king of an independent Portugal.[98]

Trusted Advisers

Some noblewomen had such clear aptitude for leadership that, even when their husbands were present, they had an active role in government. As historian Janet L. Nelson notes, queens even had a duty to advise their husbands: "While the good queen, as a woman, must acknowledge her husband's authority, she was also qualified—and obliged—to give him good counsel."[99]

Matilda, who became queen of England when she married King Henry I in 1100, showed considerable ability as a counselor and administrator for her husband:

As soon as she was married and consecrated as queen, Matilda began to take an active part in political affairs, witnessing many of Henry's charters [official documents], serving as his vice-regent when he traveled in Normandy, participating in meetings of the *curia regis* [king's council] and sitting in justice on several occasions. She also commanded vast dower lands and a large household of her own, and she exercised sufficient

patronage that several of her household officials were promoted to episcopal [bishops'] positions. Matilda was also perceived to have a great influence over Henry.[100]

Philippa of England was another wife who shared the work of government with her husband. She married King Eric of Norway, Denmark, and Sweden around

Henry I stands with his wife, Queen Matilda, who played a powerful political role in her husband's affairs.

1406, and helped him govern his wide-spread kingdom, sometimes holding council meetings for him and acting as his regent in Norway.

Philippa's popularity was an asset to Eric; even when queens and noblewomen were not directly involved in government, their acts often influenced their husbands' or sons' positions. In fulfilling her conventional role—as benefactress of a convent, for example, or in giving money or food to the poor—a noblewoman could exert influence. Christine de Pizan, writing advice for medieval women, suggested that a princess should act as "advocate and mediator between the prince her husband, or her son, if she is a widow, and her people, or all those people whom she may be able to help by doing good."[101] In her charity and care for the poor, a noblewoman could help reinforce the popularity of her husband's regime or even bring the needs of peasants to the nobleman's attention.

Combining Mercy with Strength

A famed example of a queen's intervening between the king and the people is the part played in the fourteenth-century siege of Calais by Philippa of Hainault, wife of the English king Edward III. In 1347, the king's forces besieged the city of Calais on the northern French coast. After a year the

A Fighting Woman

Sichelgaita (or Gaita) of Salerno was a twelfth-century noblewoman who joined her husband on the battlefield and earned a reputation for her fearless leadership. Anna Comnena, a Byzantine noblewomen who was seven years old at the time of Sichelgaita's death, wrote a history called *The Alexiad,* which has been translated by E.R.A. Sewter. Anna reports that Sichelgaita "went on campaign with her husband and when she donned armour was indeed a formidable sight." Sichelgaita was also known for her firmness in dealing with deserters on the battlefield:

There is a story that Robert's wife Gaita, who used to accompany him on campaign . . . seeing the runaways and glaring fiercely at them, shouted in a very loud voice: "How far will ye run? Halt! Be men!" . . . As they continued to run, she grasped a long spear and charged at full gallop against them. It brought them back to their senses and they went back to fight.

starving citizens offered to surrender on condition that they would not be harmed. King Edward, seeking revenge for the damage Calais had done to his ships, demanded that the townspeople send him six of the principal citizens, who were to come out with their heads and feet bare, ropes around their necks, and the keys of the town and the castle in their hands. Six prominent citizens duly volunteered and were led before the king, pleading for their lives. Medieval historian Jean Froissart, later Queen Philippa's secretary, recorded that though his lords, knights, and men-at-arms wept out of pity when they saw the six burghers, "the King continued to glare at them savagely, his heart so bursting with anger that he could not speak. When at last he did, it was to order their heads to be struck off immediately." [102]

Although the king's nobles and knights begged him to spare the lives of the burghers of Calais, Edward remained obstinate. His advisers pointed out that executing the six men would damage the king's reputation, giving him a name for cruelty. Still Edward refused to change his mind, perhaps fearing an appearance of weakness would diminish his authority over his barons. However, Queen Philippa then intervened, begging for mercy for the men of Calais:

The King remained silent for a time, looking at his gentle wife as she knelt in tears before him. His heart was softened, for he would not willingly have distressed her in the state she was in [she was pregnant], and at last he said: "My lady, I could wish you were anywhere else but here. Your appeal has so touched me that I cannot refuse it. So, although I do this against my will, here, take them. They are yours to do what you like with." [103]

Was Edward truly swayed by his wife's appeal, or did she provide him a way out of a difficult position? As a woman and his loyal wife, Philippa posed no threat to Edward, and he could give in to her appeal without damaging his reputation or compromising his authority. She was able to help him appear both merciful and strong as she took the six burghers of Calais, fed and clothed them, and had them escorted to safety.

Women Warriors

Throughout history, the role of warrior has belonged primarily to men. This was true in the Middle Ages, but in her study of medieval women warriors, Megan McLaughlin says that women warriors were "certainly more common than has usually been assumed." [104] McLaughlin explains that, when they were not away on crusade or fighting a distant battle, the feudal lord's band of warriors lived in the castle with the lord's family. Girls and women therefore lived alongside soldiers, heard their conversations, watched men in practice, and observed—girls may even have joined in—boys' training in the arts of war.

Through such close contact, some women acquired considerable familiarity with military matters, and were well equipped to take up arms themselves or to command a band of soldiers if necessary. In

A medieval woman dressed for battle.

The Treasure of the City of Ladies, a medieval book of advice for women, Christine de Pizan recommends that a noblewoman should learn how to fight a battle:

> We have also said that she ought to have the heart of a man, that is, she ought to know how to use weapons and be familiar with everything that pertains to them, so that she may be ready to command her men if the need arises. She should know how to launch an attack or to defend against one, if the situation calls for it. She should take care that her fortresses are well garrisoned. [105]

History tells us of a number of women who took up weapons or commanded men in battle and of the circumstances that called for women's participation in military activity.

Toughness Before Allure

Saxo Grammaticus, who wrote his *History of the Danes* around the year 1200, tells of a band of Danish women who were trained and ready for war:

> There were once women in Denmark who dressed themselves to look like men and spent almost every minute cultivating soldiers' skills; they did not want the sinews of their valor to lose tautness and be infected by self-indulgence. Loathing a dainty style

of living, they would harden body and mind with toil and endurance, rejecting the fickle pliancy of girls and compelling their womanish spirits to act with a virile ruthlessness.... As if they were forgetful of their true selves they put toughness before allure, aimed at conflicts instead of kisses, tasted blood, not lips, sought the clash of arms rather than the arm's embrace, fitted to weapons hands which should have been weaving, desired not the couch but the kill, and those they could have appeased with looks they attacked with lances. [106]

Saxo was writing not about his own time, but about an unspecified time in the past, and some historians doubt that these legendary women ever existed. Others, though, point to the fact that Viking women (from around the ninth to the eleventh century) were sometimes buried with swords and spears, suggesting that these women were warriors.

Women as highly trained warriors were, however, very unusual, and the historical record gives very few examples of medieval women who were active on the battlefield. Isabel de Montfort is one. She lived in France in the late eleventh century and was married to Ralph of Conches. A strong-willed woman, she was possibly more determined than her husband to ensure that their fiefdom was well defended. Orderic Vitalis, a twelfth-century historian, wrote that "Isabel was generous, daring, and gay, and therefore lovable and estimable to those around her. In war she rode armed as a knight among the knights; and she showed . . . courage among the knights in hauberks [tunics of chain mail] and sergeants-at-arms." [107]

A Legendary Artist and Fighter

Stories are told of another woman warrior, Oronata Rodiana, who lived in Italy and died in 1452. Historians disagree about how much of the story of her life is true. She was an artist (itself unusual for a woman) who specialized in the difficult technique of painting frescos on walls of buildings. While she was working on the palace of a lord named Gabrino Fondolo, a young nobleman attempted to rape her, but she fought him off, stabbing him. Echols and Williams record her legendary escape: "Oronata supposedly escaped to the mountains and fought with mercenary soldiers. After she was pardoned, she returned to finish Fondolo's palace." [108] Later, when her native city was under attack, she led a group of soldiers to victory, but was mortally wounded in the battle.

Joan of Arc, Commander of Soldiers

The most famous woman warrior of the Middle Ages was Joan of Arc, a young peasant Frenchwoman who stepped out-side the roles of peasant and woman to command soldiers in battle. In the early fifteenth century, the medieval region now known as France was not a single, unified country. It consisted of a number of kingdoms and dukedoms, notably Normandy, Burgundy, Armagnac, and France (at that time, a small area sur-rounding Paris), that were constantly fight-ing one another for territory and jointly facing invasion by the English in the Hundred Years' War. During Joan's child-hood the English invaded Normandy. In a treaty with the duke of Burgundy, the English king arranged for the throne of France to bypass the dauphin, or heir apparent. Many people in central and southern France were angry that the dauphin would not become king, and, coming together as Armagnac forces, they rebelled against the English invaders. Henry VI, the English king, had the sup-port of Burgundy and most of northern France.

Historian Lilas G. Edwards has des-cribed the effect that this conflict must have had on Joan's childhood:

Joan of Arc was growing up in the north-eastern province of Lorraine during these troubled years. Though far removed from the centres of power, her province had long suf-fered from the devastation of war-

Joan of Arc, a famous warrior of the Middle Ages, sits atop her horse.

fare. . . . The war undoubtedly affect-ed her life and the day-to-day lives of her family and neighbours.[109]

At the age of thirteen, Joan began to expe-rience mystical visions and to hear voices that she identified as St. Michael, St. Catherine, and St. Margaret. She believed she was called by God to help the dauphin reclaim his place as heir to the French throne. She dressed in men's clothing and persuaded the Armagnac leader to give her a band of troops, whom she led on a long journey to the dauphin's court. Winning the dauphin's trust, she prophesied that she would rescue the besieged city of Orleans and bring about his coronation. He gave her troops and arms, and she proceeded, against all odds, to fulfil her prophecies. The siege of Orleans was raised, and two months later the dauphin was crowned.

However, Joan's success ended there, and she was soon captured by Burgundian forces and sold to the English. Because of her claim that she was guided by the voices of dead saints, Joan was handed over to the church and tried in a church court for

The Order of the Hatchet

O nly men could become knights during the Middle Ages. They often belonged to organizations called orders that excluded women. Women were considered too weak to fight, and they were forbidden to dress in men's clothing or in armor.

However, the seventeenth-century historian Elias Ashmole, quoting a Spanish writer named Joseph Micheli Marquez in his chronicle *The Institution, Laws, and Ceremonies of the Most Noble Order of the Garter*, relates the story of a group of Spanish women who earned the right to belong to a special order of women knights called the Order of the Hatchet. They lived in the city of Tortosa, which belonged to the earl of Barcelona, but in 1149 it was besieged by an army of Moors (Arab Muslims). Faced with starvation, the inhabitants of Tortosa appealed to the earl for help, but his army was engaged elsewhere, and the citizens then considered surrendering.

Which the women hearing of, to prevent the disaster threatening their city, themselves, and children, put on men's clothes, and by resolute sally, forced the moors to raise the siege.

The earl, finding himself obliged, by the gallantry of the action, thought fit to make his acknowledgements thereof, by granting them several privileges and immunities; and, to perpetuate the memory of so signal an attempt, instituted an Order, somewhat like a Military Order, into which were admitted only those brave women. . . . He also ordained, that at all public meetings, the women should have precedence of the men; that they should be exempted from all taxes; and that all the apparel and jewels, though of never so great value, left by their dead husbands, should be their own.

These women . . . having thus acquired this honor by their personal valor, carried themselves after the manner of military knights of those days.

heresy (holding beliefs that were contrary to church teaching). At her trial, Joan showed the same religiously inspired courage as she did on the battlefield. Firm in the belief that the voices she heard brought instructions from God, she declared to her judges, "I am more afraid of doing wrong by saying what would displease those voices than I am to answer you." [110] She was found guilty and burned at the stake in May 1431 at the age of about nineteen.

The deeds of this peasant girl, who revived the courage of the French army and began what would eventually be a French recovery, have achieved lasting fame. Joan has long been a symbol of French national pride, and in 1920 she was finally declared a saint. However, she never made this claim for herself. In *Joan of Arc: In Her Own Words,* Willard Trask recounts an event that illustrates Joan's characteristic humility. After a significant—and seemingly miraculous—victory she was approached by a group of women who asked her to touch their rosaries (prayer beads). Joan refused, saying, "You touch them: They will be as much bettered by your touch as by mine!" [111]

Joan of Arc was a remarkable exception to the normal medieval roles of woman and of peasant, and stepped outside those conventional roles to take up a position of power. Other women who exercised power within their conventional roles were often less visible and therefore less famous, but medieval history tells us that even in a world that restricted their actions, women tested these limitations and occasionally broke them.

Chapter 6:
Women in Religion

During the Middle Ages Europe was overwhelmingly Christian, and religious belief governed daily life. In everything they did, people were conscious of God's watchful eye and concerned about what would become of their souls after death: whether they would be raised to heaven, condemned to hell, or obliged to suffer for a period in purgatory before attaining heaven. Penelope D. Johnson, a historian who has studied religious women in France, describes the Middle Ages as "a world where God and the devil were real and the absolute goal of human life was to move through its fragile earthly existence toward eternal bliss."[112]

Women shared with men this focus on the afterlife, but unlike men their only formal role in the church was as cloistered nuns in convents. As Janice Racine Norris puts it, "Christianity offered women fewer options for formal religious participation than it did men, who had opportunities as deacons, priests, canons or monks."[113] Instead, women found a variety of other ways to live out their faith.

Religion in the Home

The noblewoman was often the religious leader in the upper-class medieval household, determining when her family and servants would attend public services and influencing the household through her own example of private worship. In many cases there was a private chapel where she and her family could pray, and often a priest was part of the household or closely associated with it. It generally fell to the noblewoman, however, to decide how religion would fit into the daily life of the household.

Emphasis on religious observance varied from one household to another, with some noblewomen focusing their daily life on devotion to God. Jennifer C. Ward, who has written about medieval English noblewomen, describes the daily life of Cicely Neville, duchess of York, who was the mother of two kings, Edward IV and Richard III: "Cicely was renowned for her piety and lived what amounted to a virtually monastic life. Although time had to be set aside for public business, her day was spent in public and private devotions."[114]

A fourteenth-century painting depicts a group of noblewomen in prayer.

Almsgiving

Almsgiving, or the donation of money and goods to the poor and to the church, was an important part of medieval religious practice and one where women, through managing their households and making their wills, could exercise some influence. The church taught that God looked mercifully on those who gave to the poor. In addition, the prayers of the poor were thought to be particularly beneficial, so that if a grateful poor person prayed for the soul of a wealthy benefactor, that rich soul's time in purgatory would be reduced.

In their wills people would often leave money to the poor or to churches, monasteries, and nunneries with instructions that prayers and masses (religious services) were to be offered for the dead person's soul. Noblewomen often included relatives and sometimes servants in the list of souls to be prayed for, and the will could provide for daily prayers for decades. Ward describes one noblewoman's will:

> Joan Beauchamp, lady of Abergavenny, gave orders that she was to be buried by her husband in a new tomb in the Dominican church at Hereford. 5,000 masses were to be said for her soul as soon as possible after her death. She left 300 marks to the Dominicans at Hereford for two priests to celebrate masses for ever for the souls of her husband and herself, her parents, Sir Hugh Burnell, all her benefactors and all Christian souls. In addition, masses were to be celebrated by five honest priests for twenty years at Rochford in Essex and Kirby Bellars in Leicestershire for the souls of the same people and of her son Richard, earl of Worcester, who had died in 1422. [115]

Other wills—by both men and women—directed that money should be handed out to the poor at the church on the day of the funeral. On some occasions poor people trampled one another in the crush to get the money. Women were amongst those injured and even killed in the surging crowd. Poor women like these were desperate to feed their families, and the urgency to find food may have contributed to their willingness to offer grateful prayers on behalf of the dead benefactor.

Another way in which noblewomen of the Middle Ages fulfilled their duty to give to charity was to support a monastery or nunnery. Some women would give money or goods to a religious house, while others would pay for a new building for the monastery; these gifts were welcome, since most religious houses had few resources of their own. In many cases a noble family had a relationship with a religious house that continued for several generations, with the family making gifts while the monks or nuns would offer prayers for the family, allow the family to build a tomb in their chapel, and provide a priest who would hear family members' confessions and celebrate church sacraments such as baptism and communion. Often a noblewoman who was traveling would stay overnight at a convent, and the well-being of the religious house helped establish her reputation for generosity and good management.

As the men of the household gamble, the two women to the left tend to religious matters in this medieval painting.

Pilgrimage

Women as well as men often chose to fulfill their religious duties and express their faith by going on a pilgrimage. Throughout Europe and the Holy Land there were numerous sites that had become shrines because of their association with Jesus or a saint or because of miracles that were recorded as occurring there. Many sites contained a sacred relic, such as a piece of the cross on which Jesus was crucified, or bones, teeth, or other mummified body parts said to have belonged to a saint. During the course of the Middle Ages, millions of people made arduous journeys to these places to pray, to see the holy sites and objects for themselves, and to demonstrate their religious devotion and obedience.

Travel was slow, expensive, and hazardous in the Middle Ages. Pilgrims had to ride or walk for weeks to reach such sacred destinations as Rome in Italy, Santiago de Compostela in northwest Spain, Canterbury in England, or Jerusalem, the most holy site of all. Working people had to save for years before making these journeys, and pilgrims faced many dangers along the route. They could expect to encounter dishonest ferrymen and innkeepers, and they ran the risk of being attacked by bands of thieves. For reasons of safety, pilgrims generally traveled in groups, hoping that they would get along well with the rest of the group. Women were especially vulnerable, particularly if they took the risk of travel-

ing alone. Court records tell what happened to one woman pilgrim: "Thomas Walsham, alias Coke, late canon of Walsingham . . . raped against her will, Emma, wife of William Bode of Walsingham, coming on pilgrimage to Canterbury, and took goods . . . from her purse to the value of £20, and is a common thief." [116]

Given all these dangers, why would women undertake such journeys? Most pilgrims were curious to see for themselves the places where holy people had lived and where miraculous events took place and to pray at these sites. Many pilgrims also hoped for forgiveness for their sins or a cure for an illness. Margery Kempe, a deeply devout Englishwoman who undertook several pilgrimages and recorded them in her memoirs, hoped that making pilgrimages would win forgiveness for a grave sin that she does not specify but that weighed on her conscience. Margaret Paston, another Englishwoman who went on a pilgrimage in the 1400s, wrote to her sick husband expressing the hope that her prayerful journey would help bring him healing:

> Right worshipful husband, I recommend me to you, desiring to hear of your welfare, thanking God of the amending of the great disease that you have had. . . . I have promised to go on pilgrimage to Walsingham and to St. Leonard's Priory for you. I pray you,

Women of the Middle Ages

A painting depicts religious pilgrims as they journey to the Holy Land. Women often traveled in these pilgrimages.

send me word as hastily as you may, how your sore [illness] doeth.[117]

The desire to travel and to see far-off places was another motivation for many pilgrims, particularly for women whose everyday life was often restricted to the home itself, in contrast to men, who tended to move about, at least locally, to conduct business.

Retreat from the World

Among the women who made pilgrimages to local and far-off shrines were

On a Pilgrimage with Margery Kempe

Margery Kempe was a deeply religious woman who felt compelled to talk almost continually of her faith. Her mystical experiences caused a violent physical and emotional reaction that was sometimes seen as evidence of illness. In her memoirs (titled *The Book of Margery Kempe* and translated by John Skinner), Margery describes her outbursts:

> Sometimes . . . our Lady [the Virgin Mary] spoke in my mind; or it might otherwise be Saint Peter, Saint Paul, Saint Katherine, or whichever saint I happened to be devoted to . . . Such conversations were frequently so intimate and moved me so much by their sacredness that I would fall down, writhing and contorting both my body and face; with loud sobbings and great floods of tears I would cry out "Jesus, have mercy!" and sometimes even "I am dying!"

> It was because of all this that so many people slandered me, refusing to believe that it was the work of God. They preferred to think some evil spirit tormented my body; while others said I had some strange bodily affliction.

Margery made a number of pilgrimages during her life, sometimes traveling for months at a time. Her fellow pilgrims often found Margery's extreme piety and bizarre behavior hard to tolerate. Here Margery describes the reaction of other pilgrims when, with the permission of her confessor (or spiritual director), she gives up eating meat and living as comfortably as her traveling companions:

> In no time at all, feelings ran against me throughout our company that I no longer ate meat, and they made sure that my confessor too would be annoyed with me. But they were even more irritated by my continual tears, and the way I would speak openly all the while about the love and goodness of our Lord, both at table when we ate together as well as in other places.

Considering that the other pilgrims may not have been as deeply religious as Margery and had probably saved for years to be able to afford this once-in-a-lifetime experience, their reaction is scarcely surprising.

nuns. These women had withdrawn from the secular world to live in religious communities. They took vows of chastity and obedience; many also made a vow of poverty. Records show that convents had scant resources, and many nuns lived a harsh life, sometimes in conditions approaching starvation.

The women who became nuns were almost all from wealthy families. To be accepted into a convent, a woman had to provide a sum of money or a quantity of land similar to the dowry she would have brought to a marriage. Though the church officially prohibited these payments and attempted to prevent women from buying their way into nunneries, families still provided "gifts" to the community, and it was expected that a postulant (a candidate for entry into a religious community) would bring one. This practice had the effect of barring most poor women from convent life. In addition, poor families would be reluctant to lose a girl or woman whose labor contributed to the family's support.

One reason why women entered convent life was that, according to historian Eileen Power, nunneries "provided a career for girls of gentle [noble] birth for whom the only alternative was marriage."[118] Since social customs excluded upper-class women from professions, those who were not inclined toward marriage and motherhood could, if their families were willing, apply to enter a convent instead, and some found this life of work and prayer fulfilling.

Other women entered nunneries not because they shunned marriage, but because they had no opportunity to make a suitable match. Writing about these women, Power says, "Certainly some girls went in with no particular aptitude for religious life, and simply because there was nothing else for them to do."[119]

Of course, some women had purely religious motives for becoming nuns. They saw monastic life as the way to live out their faith, and they considered themselves "brides of Christ," giving their lives wholly to serving God through prayer and work. As Power notes, many women:

> found in the monastic environment their full spiritual fulfillment, and in doing so performed a function which rated very high in medieval estimation. Prayer and praise of God was a mode of life to which the Middle Ages attached the greatest importance . . . and in some places and at some times the nuns so serving could attain a degree of dedication and personal perfection which earned for them a renown in their lifetime and veneration by posterity.[120]

Daily Life in a Nunnery

The routine of a nun was dictated by the set of rules centered on the daily cycle of prayer services and made heavy demands on the nuns. As Power explains:

> A nun had seven monastic offices or services to say daily. She rose at 2 a.m., went down to choir for Matins, followed by Lauds, returned to bed at dawn and slept for three hours. She

got up for the day at 6 a.m. and said Prime. Tierce, Sext, None, Vespers and Compline followed at intervals through the day; the last at 7 p.m. in winter and 8 p.m. in summer, after which she was supposed to go straight to bed. All in all she got about eight hours' sleep broken in the middle by the night service. She had three meals—a light repast of bread and ale after Prime in the morning, a solid dinner to accompany reading aloud at midday and a short supper after Vespers. From 12 to 5 in winter or

Medieval nuns were required to follow a strict regular schedule for prayer, meals, and sleep.

Women of the Middle Ages

1 to 6 in summer nuns were supposed to devote themselves to work of some kind (digging, haymaking, embroidering, reading) interspersed with a certain amount of sober relaxation. [121]

The monastic rule also dictated that the nuns should remain silent, except for short periods of relaxation. It prohibited jewelry, elaborate clothing, and any pursuits that would interfere with the nuns' austere, prayerful life. It also outlined the duties of nuns, some of whom had particular responsibilities. The sacristan was in charge of the church fabrics and the lighting (by candles or lamps) throughout the community. The chambress had responsibility for the nuns' clothes, while the cellaress was in charge of food, supervised the community's servants, and ran the community's farm.

The local bishop, who had authority over monasteries in his diocese, would visit the nunnery periodically to ensure that the rules of monastic life were being followed and to attend to any business the prioress raised. Records from the later Middle Ages show that bishops often found nunneries straying from the strict rules. The most frequent faults a bishop would find were rushing through prayers and mumbling them inaudibly. But there were other distractions, such as what William of Wykeham discovered at the nunnery in Romsey in 1387:

Some of the nuns of your house bring with them to church birds, rabbits, hounds and such like frivolous things, whereunto they give more heed than to the offices of the church, with frequent hindrance to their own psalmody [singing of psalms] and that of their fellow nuns and to the grievous peril of their souls; therefore we strictly forbid you . . . to bring to church no birds, hounds, rabbits or other frivolous things that promote indiscipline; and any nun who does to the contrary, after three warnings shall fast on bread and water on one Saturday for each offence. [122]

The Monastic Economy

Each nunnery had a home farm, and nuns used their own farm produce to make bread and to brew beer. Communities of nuns employed servants, and most paid wages to a priest and a bailiff, who was in charge of daily administration. Large convents also employed a male cook, a brewer, a baker, a dairywoman, a laundress, and a porter. Nuns in small convents who had to do their own cooking and housework often complained of being overworked.

Most nunneries suffered periods of poverty, and some were constantly in debt. Sometimes natural disasters such as severe weather damaged the convent buildings and could also destroy the convent's crops. In addition, wars sometimes resulted in damage to the convent and its farmlands. Nunneries were expected to provide hospitality for nobles or even a retirement home for old noblewomen, though usually they could ill afford to do so. What often made finances worse was the incompetence of prioresses who had no aptitude for administration or were actually dishonest. Power gives the example of one prioress who kept for herself gifts that had been given to the convent and pawned the holy vessels, while "the walls and roof of the church and dorter [dormitory] and the rest of the house were in ruins."[123]

Other Lives of Faith

Some women sought to live a life of faith other than as a wife or a nun. In the late twelfth century, women in northern Europe formed religious communities that were not bound by monastic rules. These women, who became known as Beguines, lived a life of prayer and of service to the poor and sick. In Belgium some large communities evolved to become cities within cities. Ernest W. McDonnell, who has studied the Beguines, describes the communities that grew up in Liége and Ghent:

> The full-blown beguinage comprised a church, cemetery, hospital, public square, and streets and walks lined with convents for the younger sisters and pupils and individual houses for the older and well-to-do inhabitants. In the Great Beguinage at Ghent, with its walls and moats, there were at the beginning of the fourteenth century two churches, eighteen convents, over a hundred houses, a brewery, and an infirmary.[124]

The women who lived in these communities did not take vows of obedience or poverty. They remained single as long as they lived in the community, but they were free to leave whenever they wished.

Some women of faith lived in religious solitude as hermits or anchoresses outside a religious community. They may have lived far away from a nunnery, may not have been admitted for some reason, or may simply have chosen the life of a hermit. They displayed some courage since, for a woman, living alone was contrary to medieval social custom and dangerous. The isolation of some women was interrupted, however, because they gained notoriety as healers or mystics. Jutta, a German anchoress who lived at the beginning of the twelfth century, was asked to take in girls to live with her and learn from her. One of these girls, Hildegard of Bingen, went on to become a renowned writer, composer, and healer and one of the Christian faith's foremost mystics (peo-

Euphemia of Wherwell

Euphemia was abbess of the nunnery at Wherwell in England in the mid–thirteenth century. As well as showing concern for the spiritual well-being of the nuns in her care, she had a practical focus and her construction projects suggest that she had an aptitude for design. In *Medieval English Nunneries,* historian Eileen Power quotes from fourteenth-century records of the abbey:

She increased the number of the Lord's handmaids in this monastery from forty to eighty, to the exaltation of the worship of God. To her sisters, both in health and sickness, she administered the necessaries of life with piety, prudence, care and honesty. She also increased the sum allowed for garments by 12d. each. . . . She also, with maternal piety and careful forethought, built, for the use of both sick and sound, a new and large farmery [farmhouse] away from the main buildings and in conjunction with it a dorter [dormitory] and other necessary offices. Beneath the farmery she constructed a watercourse, through which a stream flowed with sufficient force to carry off all refuse that might corrupt the air. Moreover she built there a place set apart for the refreshment of the soul, namely a chapel of the Blessed Virgin, which was erected outside the cloister behind the farmery. With the chapel she enclosed a large place, which was adorned on the north side with pleasant vines and trees. On the other side, by the river bank, she built offices for various uses, a space being left in the centre, where the nuns are able from time to time to enjoy pure air. In these and in other numberless ways, the blessed mother Euphemia provided for the worship of God and the welfare of her sisters.

ple who express and inspire faith through speaking and writing of visions and mysterious religious experiences).

Women as Religious Leaders

Although the church excluded women from the priesthood and thus from positions of leadership within the church, some women, driven by the intensity of their faith to speak out in spite of the medieval expectation that women would be silent and obedient, exercised leadership roles unofficially.

As nuns, women had opportunities to become leaders of their communities. If a nun showed an aptitude for management, she might become prioress or abbess of her convent and be responsible for the day-to-day running of the community, for maintaining relations between the nuns, and for communicating with the bishop who had authority over the community. Some women even founded new orders

Saint Clare of Assisi founded her own order of nuns to emphasize her religious devotion.

of nuns. Clare of Assisi, a friend and disciple of Francis of Assisi, followed his example and founded an order of nuns patterned after his Franciscan order of priests. Bridget of Sweden, who was married at the age of thirteen and had eight children, became a nun after her husband's death. She soon set up her own order of nuns, known as the Brigittine Order, and wrote the rules these nuns were to follow.

Several Beguines rose to positions of leadership despite the opposition of church authorities who viewed the movement with suspicion and attempted to stamp it out. Margerite Porete was a French Beguine who wrote *The Mirror of Simple Souls,* a book that expressed her belief that religiously inspired people could rise to an unusual level of piety and become independent of the church. Not surprisingly, her writing was condemned by the church and she was burned at the stake in 1310. Her book, however, was translated into Latin, Italian, and English and was widely read for many centuries.

Mystics like Hildegard of Bingen became influential leaders within the church. The fact that they were women may even have been an advantage to them in an ironical way, since many people did not believe women could speak with such insight. The only explanation most people could offer for these women's inspired words was that God was truly speaking through them, and for this reason even the church authorities paid attention to their visions. Elisabeth of Schönau was a nun and a mystic who corresponded with Hildegard and whose visions and teachings were recorded by her brother, Egbert. Although she courageously criticized church leaders for their failings, her message was widely respected and she gained a reputation as a spiritual leader. Catherine of Siena's visions of Christ began when she was just six years old. She became a nun, and word of her visions and trances spread throughout Italy and beyond.

Women Outside Mainstream Religion

The Middle Ages, an era when religion dominated all aspects of people's lives, spawned a great number of dissident religious movements outside the orthodox church. These movements challenged central beliefs of the church by offering alternative ideas, and were condemned and stamped out—sometimes violently—by the church authorities. The Cathars and Waldensians in France and Spain, Hussites in eastern Europe, and Lollards in England all gained strong followings before being condemned. Some of these movements allowed women to participate in worship, preaching, and teaching, and for this reason they may have been particularly attractive to women who were searching for a way to express their faith. It is possible also that the visible role of

Two witches brew a potion, adding a snake and a chicken to a bubbling cauldron.

women in these movements added to the church's disapproval.

Throughout the Middle Ages there were also women and men who pursued a spirituality that became associated with magic. Many of these people were thought to have supernatural healing powers, but some were reputed to have powers to do evil. Toward the end of the Middle Ages this spirituality became increasingly known as witchcraft and associated with women. In 1486 two Dominican monks working for the Inquisition published a document called the *Malleus Maleficarum* (*The Hammer of Witches*). Designed to expose and punish witches, the document warns that the fact that most witches are women "is accredited by experience," and that women have a tendency to become witches because they are "feebler in mind and body" than men and because "woman is a wheedling and secret enemy."[125] This negative stereotype of women contributed to the witch-hunts that arose in the late Middle Ages and continued for many centuries.

In a world dominated by religion and ruled by men, women often had to struggle to find a role in which they could express their faith. Perhaps because they had no obvious role in the church, women's spirituality was expressed in a wide variety of ways, and it may be that the struggle for a voice intensified the faith of some women. Certainly, by the end of the medieval period women were a strong influence on religion. In spite of the restrictions they faced, religious women in the Middle Ages—as heads of households, almsgivers, nuns, and mystics—had a powerful influence on their world.

Chapter 7:
Women Writers and Artists

❧

Museums around the world hold valuable collections of medieval art and manuscripts, and many European cities are dominated by soaring medieval cathedrals. Yet tracing the part that women played in the production of these works is difficult. In the Middle Ages artworks were often produced not by a single artist but by a group working together in a workshop. Personal self-expression was not a priority for these artists, and consequently they rarely signed their work. In addition, although women worked in them, workshops were generally run by men, and where a name is known, it is usually his. Art historian David Wilkins points out that "women clearly produced works of art, but only within the collaborative and essentially anonymous situation of the medieval workshop, and we can isolate neither their particular works nor their share in the workshop's production." [126]

It is also important to notice that women of every class in medieval society worked in textile arts: weaving, tapestry, embroidery, and making ceremonial clothing and linens. However, textiles like these were in regular use in homes and church-es, and most of these women's artworks simply deteriorated over the centuries. In contrast, books, some of which were written or illustrated by women, were rare and valuable in the Middle Ages and were carefully handled, so many have survived. Some of the most famous women of the Middle Ages are known today through their writing.

Women in Literature

Few people in the Middle Ages were literate, and most of those who could read and write were men. For this reason, most medieval writing is by men and generally with a male audience in mind. These works often portray women as belonging to one of two moral extremes: as either saintly or corrupt. Nonfiction writing, such as the lives of saints, describes selfless women who dedicate themselves to God and fearlessly protect their virginity. However, writers of sermons depict women as sly temptresses who lead innocent men astray. Fictional works also present these two contradictory images. In the genre called "courtly love," knights dedicate themselves to idealized, faultless

Saintly women, the focus of the "courtly love" genres, tend sheep in a pasture.

ladies, while in the stories known as *fabliaux*, women are depicted as immoral and men are cautioned to avoid them at all costs. The writing of women themselves reaches beyond these dual stereotypes, giving glimpses into the real lives and feelings of women in the distant past.

Women Troubadours

The courtly love tradition in literature began in twelfth-century Occitania, in today's southern France. In a reversal of the feudal order, male poets—known as troubadours—wrote of themselves as vassals bound to serve a lady of perfect beauty and virtue. Women poets gave their own twist to this tradition, writing songs of love for men. This excerpt from a poem by Castelloza comments on the social customs that controlled relations between men and women:

> It greatly pleases me when people say
> that it's unseemly for a lady to
> approach a man she likes and hold him

deep in conversation; but whoever says that isn't very bright, and I want to prove before you let me die that courting brings me great relief when I court the man who's brought me grief. [127]

Marie de France

Marie de France was a writer who lived in the twelfth century. She is best known for her *Lais,* stories written in verse that illustrate different kinds of love. She also wrote a large number of verse fables that are similar to Aesop's fables. Her stories were very popular during the Middle Ages and were translated into a number of different languages, including Norwegian. Marie made sure her readers would know whose words they were reading: "At the conclusion of this work, which I have written and narrated in French, I shall name myself for posterity: Marie is my name, and I am from France. It may be that many writers will claim my work as their own, but I want no one else to attribute it to himself. He who lets himself fall into oblivion does a poor job." [128]

Earning a Living by Writing

Over two hundred years later, another French woman became famous for her

The Fox and the Eagle

Scholars believe that the twelfth-century writer Marie de France was a noblewoman and probably quite wealthy. Nevertheless, fables like "The Fox and the Eagle" (this translation is from *The Fables of Marie de France* by Mary Lou Martin) show that she had sympathy for poor people trapped within the feudal system.

A fox once went out of his hole and was playing in front of it with his young. An eagle came flying by and carried off one of them. The fox went after him, crying that he should give him back his little one, but the eagle would not listen at all, so the fox had to return home. He took a torch and went gathering kindling wood. Then he put it around the oak where the eagle had his nest. When the eagle saw the fire that had started, he begged the fox and said, "Friend, put out the fire! Take your little one! All my nestlings will surely be burned."

We see by this fable that it is likewise with the proud, rich man: he will never have mercy on the poor man because of his hue and cry, but if the poor man could wreak vengeance on him, then you would see the rich man bow.

writing. Christine de Pizan was probably the first woman in Europe to become a professional writer. She was born in Italy but moved to Paris a year later when her father was appointed court astrologer and physician to Charles V. She received an excellent education in Paris, married there, and had three children. However, her husband died when Christine was twenty-five, leaving her to support her children and her mother, so she turned to writing. At that time writers and other artists were dependent on wealthy patrons. The writer would dedicate his or her work to the patron and receive a gift of money in return. Christine's patrons included the dukes of Burgundy and Orleans.

Christine despised the popular stories that treated women so critically and wrote instead about heroic women who were morally and physically courageous. She also wrote a book of advice to women on how to behave so that they would win respect and live happily in medieval society. In that work she addresses women of all social classes and ages, giving practical advice on topics ranging from politics to clothes. At one point she discusses the problem of communication between the generations, saying, "All too frequently, debate and discord spoil the association between old people and young. In opinions as well as language, they differ enough to dislike one another as if they were two different species."[129] She then gives advice to both old and young to help them get along:

When she [the older woman] feels any antipathy to young people . . . here is how she should counsel herself: "Good Lord! You were once young yourself! Remember what things you did then. Would you have wanted to be spoken of in this way? Why are you so hard on them?" . . . The young woman should serve, respect, and revere the older one, tolerating correction with good grace if she should do anything wrong or imprudent. Never should she answer disrespectfully, but rather hold her peace, avoiding what she knows will displease. In so doing, she greatly will be praised. Therefore, if the old treat the young considerately and the young reciprocate to the old, peace will be preserved among those often in great contention, and it will endure.[130]

Two Historians

Other medieval women who wrote nonfiction works include Juliana Berners, who wrote *The Treatise of Fishing with an Angle,* and the two great medical writers, Trotula and Hildegard of Bingen. There were also two outstanding women who wrote histories of their own times. One was Anna Comnena of Byzantium, who lived from 1083 to 1153. From her father, Alexius

Christine de Pizan presents her book to Isabeau of Bavière. Although medieval woman were generally illiterate, some of them authored books.

Comnenus, she expected to inherit the vast Byzantine empire stretching from Italy to Armenia, but her hopes were dashed by the birth of her brother, John. She did everything she could to persuade her father to make her his heir, but without success, and eventually she conspired in an attempt to kill John. Exiled from court, she began work on the *Alexiad,* a history of Byzantium in which she praised her father and ignored her brother. According to Marcelle Thiébaux, who prepared a modern edition of her work, Anna's writing is vivid: "Anna provides many eyewitness accounts, along with her own and other people's conversations, whether remembered or invented. . . . There are details of court intrigues and military battles, stratagems and disguises, gougings, maimings, and public burnings." [131]

Another woman historian was Helene Kottanner. The daughter of a minor nobleman, she was born around 1400 and became an aide to Queen Elizabeth of Hungary. Maya Bijvoet Williamson, who has edited and translated Helene's writing, describes the responsibilities of Helene's position:

She was not only in charge of the queen's wardrobe and the material well-being of the ladies-in-waiting, she was also entrusted with the education of the king's children, gave council and was listened to, had a considerable impact on Queen Elizabeth's decisions, and was sent on a highly dangerous secret mission. In other words, the woman who portrays herself in these pages had a wide range of tasks and responsibilities. [132]

As a trusted adviser and friend to the queen, Helene was intimately familiar with the details of court life. In addition, her husband was employed by the king. Helene's account reflects her knowledge and understanding of the politics of the time.

Writing by Mystics

An important branch of medieval women's writing is the work of mystics, women who had visions that they believed were inspired by God. Since all church authorities were men and Christian dogma held that women were weak, unreliable, and unsuited for any church voice, these women, by claiming God's inspiration and describing their visions, were challenging the church. One of the most remarkable visionary writers was Hildegard of Bingen (1093–1179). At the relatively advanced age of forty-two, Hildegard received a com-

An illustration by Hildegard of Bingen shows man as the center of the universe.

mand to "say and write what you see and hear." Still, she wrote that she was reluctant to record her visions:

> But although I heard and saw these things, because of doubt and a low opinion (of myself) and because of the diverse sayings of men, I refused for a long time the call to write, not out of stubbornness but out of humility, until weighed down by the scourge of God, I fell into a bed of sickness. [133]

As soon as she began the task of writing, she recovered from her illness. It took her ten years to complete her great religious work, the *Scivias*. During the rest of her extraordinarily long life, Hildegard became famous throughout Europe, an adviser to popes and kings and the founder of a convent. She wrote scientific treatises about natural history, medical works about the healing properties of plants and animals, plays, and letters to religious and secular rulers such as Eleanor of Aquitaine.

Another mystic who was hesitant to write was Mechthild of Magdeburg, who lived from about 1212 to around 1282. In her intense visions she describes the relationship between God and her soul as the bond between lovers. However, she also expresses deep humility and describes herself as unworthy of her visions. As historian Gwynne Kennedy explains,

> At times she described herself as a "poor despised little woman," and "unworthy bride [of Christ]," and "unworthy soul" to receive divine communication. Yet she was also acutely aware that she was more vulnerable to persecution for her visions and writings than a man would have been. At one point, she prayed to God after being told that her book should be burned, and God reassured her that no human can burn truth. She then lamented that if she were a "learned

priest" God would instead have garnered praise for his revelations. God explained that he deliberately chose Mechthild to receive his "special grace" rather than learned men *because* of her humility. Moreover, God continued, the Church is strengthened when "unlearned lips" teach his words to "learned tongues." [134]

Since most men in the Middle Ages held a low opinion of the intelligence of women, they did not think that a woman would be capable of producing such compelling works by themselves. The very fact that mystics like Hildegard, Mechthild, and Catherine of Siena (a fourteenth-century visionary who advised popes) could speak wisely was taken as proof that they received communication from God.

Scribes and Illuminators

Until the invention of the printing press in the mid–1400s made mass production of books possible, all medieval books were manuscripts, painstakingly hand written by a scribe or copyist. Women worked as copyists, both in nunneries and, as artists' studios proliferated in the late Middle Ages, in city workshops. Some of these women were also illuminators, decorating and illustrating the books they produced.

Illuminated manuscripts—so called because of the way the gold and silver decorations would catch the light (*lumen* is Latin for light)—are among the most highly prized medieval artworks. Most illuminated manuscripts are religious works, either books of the Bible or prayer books, and the religious focus of the medieval world is revealed in the exquisite design and fine detail of the illumination, as well as in the use of silver, gold, and costly paints.

Some of the most beautiful—and most common—medieval books are so-called books of hours, collections of prayers to be recited in private at certain times of day, analogous to the monastic cycle of prayers that divided a monk's or nun's day into eight segments of communal worship. The reason so many books of hours have survived is that they were a very popular sign of religious devotion in the Middle Ages, so large numbers of them were produced. Wealthy people would commission highly decorated ones, and even families that owned no other books would try to buy a book of hours. Art historian Christopher de Hamel writes of a medieval poem that illustrates the value of a book of hours to middle-class Frenchwomen:

> The poet Eustache Deschamps (1346–1406) describes the bourgeois wife who feels she is not properly fitted out unless she owns a Book of Hours, beautifully made, illuminated in gold and blue (says the poem), neatly arranged and well painted and

bound in a pretty binding with gold clasps.[135]

Hamel also gives the example of an English owner of a book of hours who valued his book so greatly that he wrote on the flyleaf, "He that steals this book shall be hanged upon a hook behind the kitchen door."[136]

Illuminators—men and women—rarely signed their work or identified themselves, but we do know the names of some women who worked in this art form. One was Ende, a Spanish nun who worked with a monk named Emerterius in the late tenth century. Another was the German Diemudis of Wessobrun, who lived from around 1057 to 1130 and is known to have copied and illuminated forty-five manuscripts, an impressive achievement, since a

An initial "V" from an illuminated manuscript shows the tremendous detail and beauty that went into creating just one letter.

single illuminated manuscript could require more than a year's work.

Textile Arts

In all cultures, needlework is traditionally a woman's occupation, and there is evidence that women (though not only women) in the Middle Ages were closely involved in designing and creating functional and artistic embroidery and tapestries both for wealthy individuals and for the church. As David Wilkins explains:

> The most complete documentary evidence of women artists is found in the needle arts, where women are recorded as playing an important role as embroiderers, weavers, and makers of tapestries. Their activity is especially well documented in England, where the finest and most famous embroidery of the Middle Ages . . . was produced. All classes of English women seem to have been involved in this practice and works of fine quality were produced in both simple dwellings and in royal castles. [137]

Like manuscripts, pieces of needlework were rarely signed, and historians have to search account books, letters, and other documents to determine the names of textile artists. Rozsika Parker has studied all the records concerning one embroiderer:

> The name of Mabel of Bury St. Edmunds appears twenty-four times

between 1239 and 1245 in the Liberate Rolls [official records] of Henry III. For a medieval artist Mabel is well documented. She was an independent worker rather than an employee of the King's merchant suppliers. In 1239 the King ordered that she be paid £10 for embroidering a chasuble [part of a priest's vestments] and an offertory veil [an item of church linen]. The order was an important one, so the King must already have known and respected her work. Two years later pearls were purchased for Mabel to use on the chasuble, and she was given 40 shillings to buy gold. [138]

Mabel was paid by the king for numerous other pieces of embroidery, including a banner showing the Virgin Mary and St. John, where Mabel was given a free hand to design the banner herself—a tribute to her artistry. In 1256 the king made her a gift of cloth and rabbit fur for a robe, a traditional gift denoting respect.

The most famous piece of textile art dating from the Middle Ages is the Bayeux tapestry, which is not in fact a tapestry at all, since it was not created by weaving threads of different colors to form a picture, but was embroidered using silk threads on a linen cloth. It is a work of impressive size—just twenty inches high, but more than two hundred feet long—and it tells the story of the Norman invasion of England culminating in the Battle of Hastings (1066). It was worked in such detail that historians have been able to turn to it for information on armor, carts, boats, and other aspects of medieval life. Whitney Chadwick summarizes the significance of the Bayeux tapestry and the role women played in its creation:

> The only surviving example of Romanesque political embroidery of the eleventh century, the Bayeux Tapestry has been called the "most important monument of secular art of the Middle Ages." ... [Most] historians believe that it was made at an estate or nunnery, possibly in Canterbury or Winchester where embroiderers had long enjoyed royal patronage, and probably by women, as contemporary documents include no mention of male needleworkers. [139]

Music

Hildegard of Bingen, famous in her own time for her visionary writing and her

Stealing the Crown of St. Stephen

Helene Kottanner, an employee of the widowed Queen Elizabeth of Hungary, wrote a book (published as *The Memoirs of Helene Kottanner* in a translation by Maya Bijvoet Williamson), describing the events of her adventurous life. In this episode, which occurred in 1440, Helene and an accomplice work together to gain possession of the Holy Crown of St. Stephen for Queen Elizabeth's unborn baby:

> When the Holy Crown was completely free, we again closed the doors everywhere, replaced the locks . . . pressed my lady's seal on them once more, and locked the outer door again and tied the piece of cloth with the seal

on it as we had found it. ... And I threw the files in the privy in the room of the ladies, where you will find them, if you break it open, as proof that I am speaking the truth.

> We carried the Holy Crown through the chapel of Saint Elizabeth. ... Then my helper took a red velvet pillow, opened it, removed part of the feathers, put the Holy Crown into the pillow, and sewed it back up.

Helene smuggled the crown to the queen, who, within an hour, gave birth to a baby boy. Three months later the baby was crowned king of Hungary.

A detail from a fourteenth-century panal shows a trio of female musicians depicted as angels.

scientific and medical works, is best known today for her musical compositions. Inspired by her faith, she set prayers and verse to hauntingly beautiful music, in the form known as plainsong chant, that is still performed around the world. Another woman composer and performer was Catherine of Bologna, an abbess who, like Hildegard, had many other gifts, including painting. Echols and Williams write, "She also composed songs for her nuns, and is often pictured playing the viola."[140]

Since music was an accepted part of daily life both in nunneries and in homes, we can assume that many women were involved in composition and performance, from simple singers of folk songs in the home to composers of complex sacred and court music. Like so many of the illu-minators, embroiderers, and even writers, these musicians are anonymous to us, and many of their works have been lost in the intervening centuries. Yet those women writers, artists, and musicians whose names are recorded testify to the role of women in the world of medieval art.

Notes

Chapter 1: Women in the Countryside: Peasants Working at Home and in the Fields

1. Judith M. Bennett, *Women in the Medieval English Countryside.* New York: Oxford, 1987, p. 36.
2. Werner Rosener, *Peasants in the Middle Ages,* trans. Alexander Stutzer. Urbana: University of Illinois Press, 1992, p. 53.
3. Quoted in Emilie Amt, ed., *Women's Lives in Medieval Europe: A Sourcebook.* New York: Routledge, 1993, p. 183.
4. Bennett, *Women in the Medieval English Countryside,* pp. 43–44.
5. Bennett, *Women in the Medieval English Countryside,* p. 72.
6. Rosener, *Peasants in the Middle Ages*, p. 181.
7. Bennett, *Women in the Medieval English Countryside,* p. 27.
8. Quoted in Bennett, *Women in the Medieval English Countryside,* p. 6.
9. Quoted in Bennett, *Women in the Medieval English Countryside,* p. 140.
10. Barbara A. Hanawalt, "At the Margins of Women's Space in Medieval Europe," in Robert R. Edwards and Vickie Ziegler, eds., *Matrons and Marginal Women in Medieval Society.* Woodbridge: Boydell Press, 1995, p. 10.
11. Bennett, *Women in the Medieval English Countryside,* p. 121.
12. Helena Graham, "'A Woman's Work . . .': Labor and Gender in the Late Medieval Countryside," in P.J.P. Goldberg, ed., *Woman Is a Worthy Wight: Women in English Society c. 1200–1500.* Phoenix Mill, UK: Alan Sutton, 1992, p. 129.
13. Adapted from David Herlihy, *Opera Muliebria: Women and Work in Medieval Europe.* Philadelphia: Temple University Press, 1990, p. 76.
14. Marty Williams and Anne Echols, *Between Pit and Pedestal: Women in the Middle Ages.* Princeton, NJ: Markus Wiener, 1994, p. 29.
15. Kathryn Hinds, *Life in the Middle Ages. The Countryside.* New York: Benchmark, 2001, p. 41.
16. Rosener, *Peasants in the Middle Ages,* p. 214.
17. Quoted in Amt, *Women's Lives in Medieval Europe,* p. 181.

18. Adapted from Barbara A. Hanawalt, *The Ties That Bound: Peasant Families in Medieval England.* New York: Oxford University Press, 1986, p. 162.

19. Rosener, *Peasants in the Middle Ages,* p. 6.

20. Quoted in Bennett, *Women in the Medieval English Countryside,* p. 6.

Chapter 2: Women in the Towns and Cities: Skilled Workers and Business Owners

21. Rosener, *Peasants in the Middle Ages,* p. 25.

22. Maryanne Kowaleski and Judith M. Bennett, "Crafts, Gilds and Women in the Middle Ages: Fifty Years After Marian K. Dale," *Signs,* vol. 14, no. 16, 1988/89, p. 480.

23. P.J.P. Goldberg, "Female Labour, Service and Marriage in the Late Medieval Urban North," *Northern History* 22, 1986, p. 21.

24. Goldberg, "Female Labour," p. 24.

25. Ann J. Kettle, "Ruined Maids: Prostitutes and Servant Girls in Later Medieval England," in Edwards and Zieglar, *Matrons and Marginal Women,* p. 20.

26. Goldberg, "Female Labour," pp. 28–29.

27. Goldberg, "Female Labour," pp. 30–31.

28. Herlihy, *Opera Muliebria,* p. 95.

29. Herlihy, *Opera Muliebria,* pp. 143–45.

30. Shulamith Shahar, *The Fourth Estate: A History of Women in the Middle Ages,* trans. Chaya Galai. London: Methuen, 1983, p. 192.

31. Kowaleski and Bennett, "Crafts, Gilds and Women in the Middle Ages," p. 480.

32. Margret Wensky, "Women's Guilds in Cologne in the Later Middle Ages," *Journal of European Economic History,* 1982, p. 639.

33. Wensky, "Women's Guilds," p. 641.

34. Wensky, "Women's Guilds," p. 645.

35. Wensky, "Women's Guilds," p. 650.

36. Judith R. Baskin, "Medieval Jewish Women," in Linda E. Mitchell, ed., *Women in Medieval Western European Culture.* New York: Garland, 1999, p. 75.

37. Michael Adler, *Jews of Medieval England.* London: Edward Goldston, 1939, p. 39.

38. Baskin, "Medieval Jewish Women," in Mitchell, *Women in Medieval Western European Culture,* p. 75.

39. Shahar, *The Fourth Estate,* p. 194.

40. Williams and Echols, *Between Pit and Pedestal,* p. 52.

41. Edith Ennen, *The Medieval Woman.* Oxford: Basil Blackwell, 1989, pp. 166–67.

42. Goldberg, "Female Labour," p. 32.

43. Herlihy, *Opera Muliebria,* p. 191.

Chapter 3: Women in the Professions

44. Carole Rawcliffe, *Medicine and Society in Later Medieval England.* Phoenix Mill, UK: Alan Sutton, 1995, p. 72.

45. Rawcliffe, *Medicine and Society in Later Medieval England,* p. 188.

46. Joseph Shatzmiller, *Jews, Medicine, and Medieval Society.* Berkeley and Los Angeles: University of California Press, 1994, p. 109.

47. Anne Echols and Marty Williams, *An Annotated Index of Medieval Women.* New York: Markus Wiener, 1992, p. 218.

48. Herlihy, *Opera Muliebria,* p. 105.

49. Monica H. Green, ed. and trans., *The Trotula: A Medieval Compendium of Women's Medicine.* Philadelphia: University of Pennsylvania Press, 2001, p. 60.

50. Elizabeth Brooke, *Woman Healers Through History.* London: Women's Press, 1993, p. 37.

51. Brooke, *Woman Healers Through History,* p. 39.

52. Herlihy, *Opera Muliebria,* p. 107.

53. Quoted in Brooke, *Woman Healers Through History,* p. 61.

54. Quoted in Brooke, *Woman Healers Through History,* p. 77.

55. Hilary Bourdillon, *Women as Healers: A History of Women and Medicine.* Cambridge, England: Cambridge University Press, 1988, p. 15.

56. Quoted in Brooke, *Woman Healers Through History,* p. 77.

57. Shahar, *The Fourth Estate,* p. 203.

58. Rawcliffe, *Medicine and Society in Later Medieval England,* p. 187.

59. Brooke, *Woman Healers Through History,* p. 73.

60. Brooke, *Woman Healers Through History,* p. 70.

61. Bennett, *Women in the Medieval English Countryside,* p. 20.

62. Herlihy, *Opera Muliebria,* p. 115.

63. Williams and Echols, *Between Pit and Pedestal,* p. 162.

64. Bennett, *Women in the Medieval English Countryside,* p. 142.

65. Williams and Echols, *Between Pit and Pedestal,* p. 162.

66. Goldberg, *Woman Is a Worthy Wight,* p. 161.

67. Williams and Echols, *Between Pit and Pedestal,* p. 174.

68. Amy Livingstone, "Powerful Allies and Dangerous Adversaries: Noblewomen in Medieval Society," in Mitchell, *Women in Medieval Western European Culture,* p. 21.

69. Williams and Echols, *Between Pit and Pedestal,* pp. 164–65.

Chapter 4: Women Estate Administrators

70. Jennifer C. Ward, "English Noblewomen and the Local

Community in the Later Middle Ages" in Diane Watt, *Medieval Women in Their Communities*. Toronto: University of Toronto Press, 1997, p. 189.

71. Quoted in Frances and Joseph Gies, *A Medieval Family: The Pastons of Fifteenth-Century England*. New York: HarperCollins, 1998, p. 8.

72. Jennifer Ward, *English Noblewomen in the Later Middle Ages*. London: Longman, 1992, p. 7.

73. Williams and Echols, *Between Pit and Pedestal*, p. 16.

74. Williams and Echols, *Between Pit and Pedestal*, p. 24.

75. Gies, *A Medieval Family*, p. 60.

76. Gies, *A Medieval Family*, p. 137.

77. Livingstone, "Powerful Allies and Dangerous Adversaries" in Mitchell, *Women in Medieval Western European Culture*, pp. 14–15.

78. Quoted in Gies, *A Medieval Family*, p. 39.

79. Gies, *A Medieval Family*, p. 54.

80. Quoted in Rowena E. Archer, "'How Ladies . . . Who Live on Their Estates Ought to Manage Their Households and Estates: Women as Landholders and Administrators in the Later Middle Ages," in Goldberg, *Woman Is a Worthy Wight*, p. 151.

81. Archer, "How Ladies . . . Who Live on Their Estates," in Goldberg, *Woman Is a Worthy Wight*, pp. 150–51.

82. ffiona Swabey, *Medieval Gentlewoman: Life in a Gentry Household in the Later Middle Ages*. New York: Routledge, 1999, p. 11.

83. Gies, *A Medieval Family*, p. 132.

84. Ward, *English Noblewomen*, p. 23.

85. Quoted in Gies, *A Medieval Family*, p. 62.

86. Adapted from Ann S. Haskell, "The Paston Women on Marriage" in Lynn White Jr., ed., *Viator: Medieval and Renaissance Studies*, vol. 4. Berkeley and Los Angeles: University of California Press, 1973, p. 463.

87. Adapted from Haskell, "The Paston Women on Marriage," p. 463.

88. Ward, *English Noblewomen*, p. 34.

89. Quoted in Archer, "'How Ladies . . . Who Live on Their Estates," in Goldberg, *Woman Is a Worthy Wight*, p. 154.

90. Quoted in Margaret Labarge, *A Medieval Miscellany*. Ottawa: Carleton University Press, 1997, p. 105.

91. Quoted in Goldberg, *Woman Is a Worthy Wight*, p. 174.

Chapter 5: Women in Power

92. Christine Owens, "Noblewomen and Political Activity," in Mitchell, *Women in Medieval Western European Culture*, p. 210.

93. Derek Baker, Introduction to Theresa M. Vann, ed., *Queens,*

Regents, and Potentates. Women of Power series. Ghent, Belgium: Academia Press, 1995, p. 13.

94. Quoted in Lyn Reese, "Female Heroes: The Women Left Behind," *Women in World History Curriculum,* www.womeninworldhistory.com.

95. Jennifer C. Ward, "English Noblewomen and the Local Community," in Watt, *Medieval Women in Their Communities,* p. 190.

96. Christine Owens, "Noblewomen and Political Activity," in Mitchell, *Women in Medieval Western European Culture,* p. 214.

97. Echols and Williams, *An Annotated Index of Medieval Women,* p. 90.

98. Echols and Williams, *An Annotated Index of Medieval Women,* p. 400.

99. Janet L. Nelson, "Medieval Queenship," in Mitchell, *Women in Medieval Western European Culture,* p. 193.

100. Lois L. Huneycutt, "Intercession and the High-Medieval Queen: The Esther Topos," in Jennifer Carpenter and Sally-Beth MacLean, eds., *Power of the Weak: Studies on Medieval Women.* Urbana: University of Illinois Press, 1995, p. 133.

101. Quoted in Nelson, "Medieval Queenship," in Mitchell, *Women in Medieval Western European Culture,* pp. 200–201.

102. Jean Froissart, *Chronicles,* ed. and trans. Geoffrey Brereton. New York: Penguin Books, 1978, p. 108.

103. Froissart, *Chronicles,* p. 109.

104. Megan McLaughlin, "The Woman Warrior: Gender, Warfare, and Society in Medieval Europe," *Women's Studies* 17, 1990, p. 196.

105. Quoted in McLaughlin, "The Woman Warrior," p. 203.

106. Quoted in McLaughlin, "The Woman Warrior," pp. 194–95.

107. Orderic Vitalis, *The Ecclesiastical History of Orderic Vitalis,* vol. 4, ed. and trans. Marjorie Chibnall. Oxford: Clarendon Press, 1969, p. 213.

108. Echols and Williams, *An Annotated Index of Medieval Women,* p. 358.

109. Lilas G. Edwards, "Joan of Arc: Gender and Authority in the Text of the *Trial of Condemnation,*" in Katherine J. Lewis, James Menuge, and Kim M. Phillips, eds., *Young Medieval Women.* New York: St. Martin's, 1999, p. 134.

110. Joan of Arc, *Joan of Arc: In Her Own Words,* ed. and trans. Willard Trask. New York: BOOKS & Co., 1996, p. 96.

111. Joan of Arc, *Joan of Arc: In Her Own Words,* p. 73.

Chapter 6: Women in Religion

112. Penelope D. Johnson, *Equal in Monastic Profession: Religious Women in Medieval France.* Chicago:

University of Chicago Press, 1991, p. 2.

113. Janice Racine Norris, "Nuns and Other Religious: Women and Christianity in the Middle Ages" in Mitchell, *Women in Medieval Western European Culture,* p. 287.

114. Ward, *English Noblewomen,* p. 145.

115. Ward, *English Noblewomen,* p. 151.

116. Quoted in Edith Rickert, Clair C. Olson, and Martin M. Crow, eds., *Chaucer's World.* New York: Columbia University Press, 1948, p. 257.

117. Quoted in Marjorie Rowling, *Life in Medieval Times.* New York: Berkley, 1968, p. 94.

118. Eileen Power, *Medieval Women.* Cambridge, England: Cambridge University Press, 1995, p. 81.

119. Power, *Medieval Women,* p. 82.

120. Power, *Medieval Women,* p. 82.

121. Power, *Medieval Women,* p. 85.

122. Quoted in Eileen Power, *Medieval English Nunneries,* New York: Biblo and Tannen, 1964, p. 307.

123. Power, *Medieval English Nunneries,* p. 86.

124. Ernest W. McDonnell, *The Beguines and Beghards in Medieval Culture with Special Emphasis on the Belgian Scene.* New Brunswick, NJ: Rutgers University Press, 1954, p. 409.

125. Quoted in Elspeth Whitney, "Witches, Saints and Other 'Others': Women and Deviance in Medieval Culture," in Mitchell, *Women in Medieval Western European Culture,* p. 301.

Chapter 7: Women Writers and Artists

126. David Wilkins, 'Woman as Artist and Patron in the Middle Ages and the Renaissance,' in Douglas Radcliff-Umstead, ed., *The Roles and Images of Women in the Middle Ages and Renaissance.* Publications on the Middle Ages and Renaissance, vol. 3, Pittsburgh: University of Pittsburgh Press, 1975, p. 109.

127. Meg Bogin, *The Women Troubadours.* New York: Paddington Press, 1976, p. 119.

128. Marie de France, *The Fables of Marie de France: An English Translation,* trans. Mary Lou Martin. Birmingham: Summa, 1984, p. 253.

129. Christine de Pizan, *A Medieval Woman's Mirror of Honor: The Treasure of the City of Ladies,* trans. Charity Cannon Willard. New York: Persea Books, 1989, p. 203.

130. de Pizan, *A Medieval Woman's Mirror of Honor,* pp. 205, 209.

131. Marcelle Thiébaux, ed. and trans., *The Writings of Medieval Women: An Anthology,* 2nd ed. New York: Garland, 1994, p. 228.

132. Helene Kottanner, *The Memoirs of Helene Kottanner (1439–1440)*, trans. Maya Bijvoet Williamson Cambridge, England: D.S. Brewer, 1998, p. 2.

133. Quoted in Sabina Flanagan, *Hildegard of Bingen, 1098–1179: A Visionary Life.* New York: Routledge, 1989, p. 4.

134. Gwynne Kennedy, "Mechthild of Magdeburg," in Carole Levine et al., *Extraordinary Women of the Medieval and Renaissance World.* Westpoint, CT: Greenwood Press, 2000, p. 205.

135. Christopher de Hamel, *A History of Illuminated Manuscripts.* Boston: David R. Godine, 1986, p. 159.

136. de Hamel, *A History,* p. 185.

137. Wilkins, "Woman as Artist and Patron," in Radcliffe-Umstead, *Roles and Images of Women,* p. 109.

138. Rozsika Parker, *The Subversive Stitch: Embroidery and the Making of the Feminine.* New York: Routledge, 1989, p. 73.

139. Whitney Chadwick, *Women, Art, and Society.* New York: Thames and Hudson, 1997, p. 48.

140. Echols and Williams, *An Annotated Index,* p. 98.

For Further Reading

Gary L. Blackwood, *Life in a Medieval Castle.* San Diego: Lucent Books, 2000. Describes the history, purpose, and construction of medieval castles and life inside the castle walls.

Hilary Bourdillon, *Women as Healers: A History of Women and Medicine.* Cambridge, England: Cambridge University Press, 1988. Discusses women and medical practice from earliest times to the present, and has a detailed chapter on the Middle Ages. Has many illustrations drawn from contemporary books, art, and sculpture.

Polly Schoyer Brooks, *Queen Eleanor, Independent Spirit of the Medieval World.* New York: J. B. Lippincott, 1983. A short biography of Eleanor of Aquitaine. Includes illustrations, most of which are from medieval manuscripts.

Kathryn Hinds, *Life in the Middle Ages: The City.* New York: Benchmark, 2001. Information on the government of medieval cities as well as on work, childhood, games, feast days, and other topics.

————, *Life in the Middle Ages: The Countryside.* New York: Benchmark Books, 2001. Beautifully illustrated.

Gives many details of life in the villages and farms of the Middle Ages.

William W. Lace, *The Hundred Years' War.* San Diego: Lucent Books, 1994. Describes the conflicts that made up the Hundred Years' War and the war's effects on European life.

Vicki Léon, *Outrageous Women of the Middle Ages.* New York: John Wiley & Sons, 1998. Thumbnail sketches of medieval women from around the world. Includes some women from earlier and later eras as well.

Gwyneth Morgen, *Life in a Medieval Village.* Cambridge, England: Cambridge University Press, 1975. Uses contemporary art and detailed drawings to illustrate many aspects of village life, from spinning with a distaff to using medieval agricultural tools.

Don Nardo, *Life on a Medieval Pilgrimage.* San Diego: Lucent Books, 1996. Describes the conditions pilgrims experienced and their motives for making these hazardous journeys.

Sheila Sancha, *The Luttrell Village: Country Life in the Middle Ages.* New York: Crowell, 1982. Based on a real English village, this book illustrates the crofts, fields, and agricultural practices of the Middle Ages.

Internet Sources

Annenberg/CPB Learner.org, "What Was It Really Like to Live in the Middle Ages?" 1997–2002. www.learner.org. This site has sections on feudal life, religion, homes, clothing, health, the arts, and town life.

"The Middle Ages: A Medieval Fiefdom," 1995–2002. http://library.thinkquest.org. Has pages on many aspects of life in the Middle Ages, from peasants to lords and ladies.

Spartacus Educational, "The Medieval World," 2002. http://www.spartacus.schoolnet.co.uk. Provides medieval illustrations of tools, armor, and many other elements of medieval life.

Sound Recordings

Hildegard of Bingen, *A Feather on the Breath of God.* Performed by Gothic Voices. London: Hyperion, 1986. A selection of Hildegard's Latin hymns and chants; notes include Latin text with English translation.

———, *O Jerusalem.* Performed by Sequentia. New York: Deutsche Harmonia Mundi, 1997. A collection of Hildegard's music for daily services; notes include Latin text with English translation.

———, *Ordo Virtutum.* Performed by Sequentia. New York: Deutsche Harmonia Mundi, 1998. Hildegard's plainchant; notes include Latin text with English translation.

———, *Voice of the Blood.* Performed by Sequentia. New York: Deutsche Harmonia Mundi, 1995. A collection of vocal and instrumental music by Hildegard.

Works Consulted

Books

Michael Adler, *Jews of Medieval England.* London: Edward Goldston, 1939. Presents information on many Jewish women throughout England, including their marriage settlements, dowries, conflicts with the law, and business dealings.

Emilie Amt, ed., *Women's Lives in Medieval Europe: A Sourcebook.* New York: Routledge, 1993. Includes helpful introductions and extensive original sources on beliefs, customs, marriage, the noble life, the working life, and related topics.

Elias Ashmole, *The Institution, Laws, and Ceremonies of the Most Noble Order of the Garter.* London: Thomas Dring, 1693. This illustrated history of orders of knighthood includes a section on the women knights of the Order of the Hatchet.

Judith M. Bennett, *Women in the Medieval English Countryside.* New York: Oxford University Press, 1987. Uses an analysis of the court rolls of the demesne manor of Brigstock, England, to study women and work before the Black Death.

Judith M. Bennett et al., *Sisters and Workers in the Middle Ages.* Chicago: University of Chicago Press, 1989. These articles discuss crafts and gilds, prostitution, reading and books, and other topics on the lives of medieval women.

Meg Bogin, *The Women Troubadours.* New York: Paddington Press, 1976. A collection of poems (with English translations) by these medieval women of southern France. Includes an explanation of the historical and literary background.

Elizabeth Brooke, *Woman Healers Through History.* London: Women's Press, 1993. Gives extensive information on women physicians, with long quotes from the writings of Trotula and Hildegarde, among others.

Jennifer Carpenter and Sally-Beth MacLean, eds., *Power of the Weak: Studies on Medieval Women.* Urbana: University of Illinois Press, 1995. Academic essays on medieval women in history, literature, and art.

Whitney Chadwick, *Women, Art, and Society.* New York: Thames and Hudson, 1997. This influential work on women artists and the portrayal of women in art includes material on the Middle Ages.

Anna Comnena, *The Alexiad of Anna Comnena*. Trans., E.R.A. Sewter. Baltimore: Penguin Books, 1969. This work of praise for the Byzantine emperor Alexius Comnenus and history of his empire was written by his daughter, Anna, who was born in 1083.

Anne Echols and Marty Williams, *An Annotated Index of Medieval Women*. New York: Markus Wiener, 1992. Thumbnail sketches of hundreds of medieval women, with bibliographical information.

Robert R. Edwards and Vickie Ziegler, eds., *Matrons and Marginal Women in Medieval Society*. Woodbridge: Boydell Press, 1995. A collection of academic essays with a feminist focus on women's ability to act under the challenging circumstances of medieval life.

Edith Ennen, *The Medieval Woman*. Oxford: Basil Blackwell, 1989. Gives detailed information on medieval women's lives and roles, with a focus on Germany.

Sabina Flanagan, *Hildegard of Bingen, 1098–1179: A Visionary Life*. New York: Routledge, 1989. An account of Hildegard's life as nun and abbess, scientist, healer, poet, musician, theologian, and adviser to popes and rulers.

Jean Froissart, *Chronicles*. Ed. and trans. Geoffrey Brereton. New York: Penguin Books, 1978. Translation of selected passages from the writings of the noted fourteenth-century French historian.

Frances and Joseph Gies, *A Medieval Family: The Pastons of Fifteenth-Century England*. New York: HarperCollins Publishers, 1998. Describes this dynamic family in its historical and social setting and brings their story to life.

P.J.P. Goldberg, *Woman Is a Worthy Wight: Women in English Society c. 1200–1500*. Phoenix Mill, UK: Alan Sutton, 1992. Essays on medieval women and marriage, work, charity, and religious beliefs.

———, *Women in England c. 1275–1525: Documentary Sources*. Manchester: Manchester University Press, 1995. An introduction on women's lives, with original sources on the stages of life, work in the country and town, and other topics.

Monica H. Green, ed. and trans., *The Trotula: A Medieval Compendium of Women's Medicine*. Philadelphia: University of Philadelphia Press, 2001. A modern edition of this medieval medical text, with an analytical introduction on the author and her culture.

———, *Women's Healthcare in the Medieval West*. Aldershot: Ashgate Variorum, 2000. A discussion of medieval medical texts and health care practices.

Christopher de Hamel, *A History of Illuminated Manuscripts.* Boston: David R. Godine, 1986. Describes the production of illuminated manuscripts and the way they were used in the Middle Ages. Includes numerous illustrations.

Barbara A. Hanawalt, *The Ties That Bound: Peasant Families in Medieval England.* New York: Oxford University Press, 1986. Discusses the peasant way of life, including family issues, the contribution of women to the economy, stages of life, and the ways that medieval people cared for each other.

David Herlihy, *Opera Muliebria: Women and Work in Medieval Europe.* Philadelphia: Temple University Press, 1990. A study of women's work, starting in the late Roman Empire, based on records of agricultural and textile work, doctors, lawyers, preachers, and tax records of occupations in Paris.

Joan of Arc, *Joan of Arc: In Her Own Words.* Ed. and trans. Willard Trask. New York: BOOKS & Co., 1996. A selection of extracts from letters, trial records, and other documents, arranged in chronological order.

Penelope D. Johnson, *Equal in Monastic Profession: Religious Women in Medieval France.* Chicago: University of Chicago Press, 1991. A study of the nunneries of medieval France and the lives of the women within them.

Margery Kempe, *The Book of Margery Kempe.* Trans. John Skinner. New York: Image Books, 1998. The autobiography of a devout Englishwoman of the fifteenth century includes her accounts of pilgrimages.

Julius Kirshner and Suzanne F. Wemple, eds., *Women of the Medieval World.* Oxford: Basil Blackwell, 1985. Articles drawing on medieval literature as well as factual records discuss the status of women, women in religious roles, and many other topics.

Helene Kottanner, *The Memoirs of Helene Kottanner (1439–1440).* Trans. Maya Bijvoet Williamson. Cambridge, England: D.S. Brewer, 1998. A translation of the memoirs of a remarkable woman who was a trusted employee and friend of the queen of Hungary.

Margaret Labarge, *A Medieval Miscellany.* Ottawa: Carleton University Press, 1997. This collection of essays was printed to honor one of the first modern scholars to study documents revealing details about the lives of medieval women.

Carole Levine et al., *Extraordinary Women of the Medieval and Renaissance World.* Westpoint, CT: Greenwood Press, 2000. Portraits of a variety of women and descriptions of their wide-ranging achievements.

Katherine J. Lewis, James Menuge, and Kim M. Phillips, eds., *Young Medieval Women*. New York: St. Martin's, 1999. A collection of academic essays analyzing the legal and social position of young women in the Middle Ages.

Marie de France, *The Fables of Marie de France: An English Translation*. Trans. Mary Lou Martin. Birmingham: Summa, 1984. A collection of Marie de France's verse stories translated into English prose.

Ernest W. McDonnell, *The Beguines and Beghards in Medieval Culture with Special Emphasis on the Belgian Scene*. New Brunswick, NJ: Rutgers University Press, 1954. A detailed study of the men and women who made up the religious communities known as beguinages.

Linda E. Mitchell, ed., *Women in Medieval Western European Culture*. New York: Garland, 1999. A collection of essays on the law, politics, urban work, Christianity, and culture.

Baron de Montreuil, *The Life of Saint Zita, a Servant-Girl of Lucca, in the Thirteenth Century*. Trans Fr. F.X. Charlevoix. New York: P. O'Shea, 1859. Has a devotional focus; nevertheless, gives one of the few portraits of a poor city worker in the Middle Ages.

Rozsika Parker, *The Subversive Stitch: Embroidery and the Making of the Feminine*. New York: Routledge, 1989. This feminist study of the art of embroidery includes information on medieval woman needleworkers.

Christine de Pizan, *A Medieval Woman's Mirror of Honor: The Treasure of the City of Ladies*. Trans. Charity Cannon Willard. New York: Persea Books, 1989. Advice to women from all walks of life written by an independent medieval woman, probably Europe's first professional woman writer.

Eileen Power, *Medieval English Nunneries*. New York: Biblo and Tannen, 1964. A detailed study of English convents and nuns in the Middle Ages.

———, *Medieval Women*. Cambridge, England: Cambridge University Press, 1995. A study of the social conditions of women in the Middle Ages.

Douglas Radcliffe-Umstead, ed., *The Roles and Images of Women in the Middle Ages and Renaissance*. Publications on the Middle Ages and Renaissance, vol. 3. Pittsburgh: University of Pittsburgh, 1975. A collection of academic essays on women in history, art, and literature, including a study of medieval women artists and patrons.

Carole Rawcliffe, *Medicine and Society in Later Medieval England*. Phoenix Mill, UK: Alan Sutton, 1995. A history of medieval medical practice, with information on women's roles and limitations.

Zvi Razi, *Life, Marriage, and Death in a Medieval Parish.* Cambridge: Cambridge University Press, 1980. A study of the records of Halesowen, a medieval English manor.

Edith Rickert, Clair C. Olson, and Martin M. Crow, eds., *Chaucer's World.* New York: Columbia University Press, 1948. Depicts the lives and social customs of English people in the fourteenth century.

Werner Rosener, *Peasants in the Middle Ages.* Trans. Alexander Stutzer. Urbana: University of Illinois Press, 1992. A study of peasant life and the medieval rural economy.

Marjorie Rowling, *Life in Medieval Times.* New York: Berkley, 1968. Chapters on various aspects of medieval life, including one on the lives of women.

Shulamith Shahar, *The Fourth Estate: A History of Women in the Middle Ages.* Trans. Chaya Galai. London: Methuen, 1983. An analysis of medieval women's lives, with an emphasis on the challenges they faced.

Joseph Shatzmiller, *Jews, Medicine, and Medieval Society.* Berkeley and Los Angeles: University of California Press, 1994. Sets the contributions of Jews to medieval health care into the context of the culture of the time.

ffiona Swabey, *Medieval Gentlewoman: Life in a Gentry Household in the Later Middle Ages.* New York: Routledge, 1999. Presents an imaginative portrait of Dame Alice de Bryene, based on her household accounts and other records.

Marcelle Thiébaux, ed. and trans., *The Writings of Medieval Women: An Anthology.* 2nd ed. New York: Garland, 1994. A wide-ranging collection of the poetry and prose of queens, troubadours, nuns, and mystics.

Erica Uitz, *The Legend of Good Women: Medieval Women in Towns and Cities.* Mt. Kisco, NY: Moyer Bell, 1988. Presents extensive information on the roles of medieval women, with many illustrations drawn from medieval sources.

Theresa M. Vann, ed., *Queens, Regents, and Potentates.* Women of Power series. Ghent, Belgium: Academia Press, 1993. Academic essays on the lives and actions of prominent women of the Middle Ages.

Orderic Vitalis, *The Ecclesiastical History of Orderic Vitalis.* Ed. and trans. Marjorie Chibnall. Oxford: Clarendon Press, 1969. Gives the original Latin and an English translation of the historical writings of a twelfth-century monk.

Jennifer Ward, *English Noblewomen in the Later Middle Ages.* London: Longman, 1992. A study of this small but very influential group of medieval women.

Diane Watt, *Medieval Women in Their Communities.* Toronto: University of

Toronto Press, 1997. A collection of academic essays discussing the role of medieval women in the places where they lived.

Lynn White Jr., ed, *Viator: Medieval and Renaissance Studies.* Vol. 4. Berkeley and Los Angeles: University of California Press, 1973. Articles on a wide range of medieval topics, with a section on marriage in the Middle Ages.

Marty Williams and Anne Echols, *Between Pit and Pedestal: Women in the Middle Ages.* Princeton, NJ: Markus Wiener, 1994. A history of medieval women with information on individuals from many places in Europe.

Periodicals

P.J.P. Goldberg, "Female Labour, Service and Marriage in the Late Medieval Urban North" in *Northern History* 22, 1986. Draws on a wide range of records to analyze how women earned their living in northern England.

Maryanne Kowaleski and Judith M. Bennet, "Crafts, Gilds, and Women in the Middle Ages: Fifty Years After Marian K. Dale" in *Signs* 14, 1988/89. This article builds on earlier scholarship to analyze women's participation in medieval economic life.

Megan McLaughlin, "The Woman Warrior: Gender, Warfare, and Society in Medieval Europe," *Women's Studies* 17, 1990. An analysis of the part women played in medieval conflicts and of medieval attitudes toward women warriors.

Margret Wensky, "Women's Guilds in Cologne in the Later Middle Ages," *Journal of European Economic History,* 1982. Gives extensive detail on the silk makers, their guild organizations, and their businesses.

Internet Sources

Catholic Online Saints, "St. Zita," 1998–2002. saints.catholic.org.

Eternal Word Network, "St. Zita, Virgin," 2002. www.ewtn.com.

Lyn Reese, "Female Heroes: The Women Left Behind," *Women in World History Curriculum,* www.women inworldhistory.com.

Index

surgeons and barbers, 43–44
two approaches to, 43
Henry I (king of England), 73
Henry II (king of England), 70
Henry III (king of England), 58, 103
Henry IV (king of England), 50, 71
Henry VI (king of England), 62, 78
herbalists and apothecaries, 48
herbal medicine, 13, 43, 48
hermits, 90
Hersende, 46
Hildegard of Bingen
influence of, 92
medical writings of, 48, 98
musical compositions by, 104–105
visionary writings of, 90–91, 100–101
Hippocrates, 43
Holy Land, 12, 84
horoscope, 14
Horsford, Alice, 40
hospitality, 65
hospitals, 50–52
household management, 56–60
housekeeping jobs, 29
Hove, Tryngen Ime, 38
hucksters, 32, 36
humors, bodily, 43
Hundred Years' War, 12, 62, 78
husbandry, 21
Hussites, 93

illness, 9, 43
illuminated manuscripts, 101–103
illuminators, 102–103
indentures, 30
indulgences, 12

Jerusalem, 84
Jewish women, 38, 40
Joan of Arc, 77–80
jobs, skills for, 31
journeymen, 30
journeywomen, 30
Jutta, 90

Kempe, Margery, 84, 86

kempsters, 36
kings, 11, 69
kitchen, in manor estate, 57
knights
in feudal hierarchy, 11
women, 79
Knyvet, Alice, 71
Kottanner, Helene, 99–100

landowners. *See* noblemen; noblewomen
Latin, 45
laundress, 32
lawyers, 43, 52
leather crafters, 35
Lecavella, Mabilia, 40
lepers, 51–52
Licoricia of Winchester, 38, 40
life expectancy
for babies and children, 9, 19
for men and women, 8–9, 17–18, 19
linen thread, 24, 35–36
literature
fiction, 95–97
historical, 98–100
nonfiction, 98–100
poems, 95–97
portrayal of women in, 95–96
Lollards, 93
lords, 11
Louis VII (king of France), 70
Louis IX (king of France), 46
Lucca, Italy, 39
Lutzenkirchen, Fygen, 37–38
Lutzenkirchen, Lysbeth, 38

Mabel of Bury St Edmunds, 103
magic powers, 13–14, 93–94
Mahaut of Artois, 72
malnutrition, 9
maltsters, 36
manorial courts, 52–55
manorial survey, 18–19
manors, 17
see also estate administration; estates
manuscripts, 101–103
marriage

security of, 27
social status of, 25
serving maid, 26
sheep, 24
shepsters, 32, 36
shrines, 84
Sichelgaita of Salerno, 74
silk makers, 35–38
slaves, 11, 25
spinners, 35
spinsters, 31, 32, 36
spirituality, 93–94
starvation, 9
St. Patrick, 11
St. Zita of Lucca, 39
superstitions, 13–14
surgeons and barbers, 43–44
surnames, meaning of, 19, 36

tapestries, 103
tapsters, 36
textile arts, 95, 103–104
textiles, 24–25, 33
Theresa (countess of Portugal), 72–73
throwsters, 35, 36
traders, 35
Treatise of Fishing with an Angle, The (Berners), 98
Trotula of Salerno, 44, 46–48, 98

university education, 44–45
urine, 43, 44

Viking women, 77

wages, 25
Waldensians, 93
warriors
in Denmark, 76–77
famous women, 77–80
training of, 75–76
wars

financing, 62
noblemen's role in, 62
see also individual wars
Wars of the Roses, 62
water, transporting, 22
weavers, 33, 35
weaving, 24–25
websters, 36
widows, noblewomen, 71–73
wills, 82–83
winnowing, 24
witchcraft, 94
wives
beating of, 15
as legal advocates, 53–54
legal status of, 15
marital conflicts and, 20
mothers, 9, 19
women
business skills, 33–34, 40–41
in Germany, 35–38
historical research on, 16
inferior status of, 14, 15, 94
Jewish, 38, 40
lack of choices for, 41–42
legal status of, 15, 53
literary skills, 16
mothers, 9, 19
negative stereotyping of, 94
in Paris, 34–35
physical examinations of, 49
pilgrimages by, 84–87
significant contributions by, 15–16
in skilled crafts and trades, 29, 33–42
societal attitudes toward, 14, 15, 94
writing skills, 16
see also noblewomen; queens; wives
writers
famous women, 97–100
historians, 98–100
mystics, 100–101
poets, 96–97

Picture Credits

About the Authors

Ruth Dean is the president of the Writing Toolbox in Akron, Ohio. She writes books and articles and does research projects for health care organizations. She has taught English composition at the University of Akron and worked as a tutor in its Writing Center.

Melissa Thomson has a doctorate from Trinity College, Dublin, and taught seventh grade before moving to the United States. She and Ruth have written two other Lucent books, *Teen Prostitution* and *Life in the American Colonies*.